❧ Religious Symbols and God ❧

Religious Symbols and God

A Philosophical Study
of Tillich's Theology

William L. Rowe

THE UNIVERSITY OF CHICAGO PRESS
CHICAGO AND LONDON

Library of Congress Catalog Card Number: 68–16715
The University of Chicago Press, Chicago 60637
The University of Chicago Press, Ltd., London W.C. 1
Published 1968. Printed in the United States of America

To Betty, Susan, John, and Norman

Acknowledgments

The Journal of Religion has kindly given me permission for the use of parts of my article "The Meaning of 'God' in Tillich's Theology," published in 1962 (vol. 42, no. 4); and *The Monist* has permitted me to incorporate in Chapter IV part of my article "Tillich's Theory of Signs and Symbols," published in 1966 (vol. 50, no. 4). I am very grateful to the Purdue Research Foundation for two generous summer grants which made it possible for me to complete this study. A number of philosophers and theologians, both teachers and colleagues, have helped me in my philosophical work and, directly or indirectly, influenced my judgments in this study. In particular I wish to express my gratitude to William P. Alston, Charles E. Caton, Walter Kaufmann, Norman Kretzmann, Perry D. LeFevre, Bernard M. Loomer, George Nakhnikian, and Calvin O. Schrag.

Contents

Introduction

THERE are two ways of approaching the complex mind of Paul Tillich. One way is to view him as a theologian writing a theology for the Christian church in our time. A second way is to view him as a philosopher seeking to provide a comprehensive interpretation and explanation of the religious dimension of human existence. Neither approach is incorrect, for Tillich is both a Christian theologian serving the church and a speculative philosopher seeking to understand the phenomena of religion.

Since the approach taken in this book is largely of the second sort, it may be useful here to take a brief look at Tillich in his theological role.

Tillich believes that a theology must serve a particular purpose. In fact, he uses his statement of the aim or purpose of a theology not only as a guide to his own theologizing, but also as a criterion for evaluating various theological movements.

A theological system is supposed to satisfy two basic needs: the statement of the truth of the Christian message and the interpretation of this truth for every new generation. Theology moves back and forth between two poles, the eternal truth of its foundation and the temporal situation in which the eternal truth must be received. Not many theological systems have been able to balance these two demands perfectly. Most of them either sacrifice elements of the truth or are not able to speak to the situation.[1]

Two points are made here: (1) a satisfactory theology must state the eternal truth and relate this truth to the contemporary situation; and (2) most theological systems have not achieved this aim and are consequently unsatisfactory. If we ask what right has Tillich to decide what the aim of theology must be, what basic needs a theology must fulfill, his reply would be that whatever else a theology is, it is fundamentally a function of the Christian church, and therefore must serve the needs of the church. On its intellectual side the basic needs of the Christian church, Tillich contends, are two: first, the clear, precise statement of the Christian message—which the church accepts as the eternal truth—and, secondly, the statement of the bearing of this message or eternal truth on man's contemporary situation. Thus Tillich thinks he is justified in criticizing other theologies for failing to fulfill these two basic needs since he believes that they are not derived from his own predilections, but from the nature of the Christian church. Well, granted that Tillich may have some objective grounds for claiming that the aim of a theology is to fulfill these two basic needs, how is he able to employ this aim in showing other theologies to be unsatisfactory and inadequate? Tillich uses this aim of theology as a weapon against three contemporary theological movements: fundamentalism, liberalism, and the kind of

---

[1] Paul Tillich, *Systematic Theology*, 3 vols. (Chicago: University of Chicago Press, 1951–63), 1:3. Hereafter references to this work will appear in the text abbreviated as ST.

neo-orthodox theology developed by Karl Barth. By considering his criticisms of these three movements we shall have a clearer picture of what he endeavors to accomplish in his own theology.

Against *fundamentalism* as a theological movement, Tillich claims that it fails to fulfill both of the needs of a theology—it fails both to state the eternal truth and to speak to the contemporary situation. It fails to state the eternal truth because it identifies that eternal truth with a temporal expression of the truth—namely, the words of the Bible. And precisely because fundamentalism identifies the eternal truth with the literal understanding of something given in the past—the Bible—fundamentalism is unable to speak to the contemporary situation. At this point we must get clear just what Tillich means when he speaks of the 'contemporary situation.' What he does not mean is the psychological state of mind or sociological state of affairs in which most of us live. For fundamentalism can easily point to the fact that its theology is eagerly received today just because of the psychological and sociological situation in which men are living. Witness the eagerness with which men receive the theology expressed in the sermons of Billy Graham. Tillich is well aware that in periods of great personal anxiety and national stress an other-worldly theology such as is expressed in fundamentalism gains in popularity, just as he is aware that in periods of national tranquillity and personal calm a theology such as liberalism, which interprets the kingdom of God in terms of human progress and the growth of democracy, becomes popular and speaks to man's psychological and sociological state. It is not the popularity of a theology that determines its relevance to the 'present situation.'

What Tillich means by 'present situation' is the *interpretations* of human life and existence given by the nontheological disciplines. The 'situation' refers to the scientific, philosophical, economic, political, and artistic interpretations of human life and existence. Tillich is contending that a theology is inadequate if it fails to relate the eternal truth to these nontheological interpretations of human existence. Just what the nature of this *relationship* between the Christian message and the situation is cannot be developed here. This much can be said: Theology, in Tillich's view, is *not* to relate the Christian message to the contemporary situation by trying to use the Christian message to answer questions of the sort that can be answered by the situation itself. This is what fundamentalism has done. By identifying the eternal truth with a literal interpretation of the words of the Bible, fundamentalism has transformed the Biblical myths—the creation and fall of man, the virgin birth, the physical resurrection—into quasi-scientific hypotheses and put them forth as answers to questions of the sort which the situation (the nontheological disciplines) can answer for itself. As a result theology ceases to be related to the situation; instead it enters into a losing battle with science and philosophy, to which the past four centuries bear witness. Thus Tillich regards the theology of fundamentalism as failing to fulfill either of the two basic aims of a theology.

Against *liberalism* as a theological movement, Tillich claims that it has failed to grasp the Christian message; instead, it has *reduced* the eternal truth of the Christian message to certain aspects of the contemporary situation. Dewey, for example, reduced the meaning of the term

'God' to certain ideals we posit and certain natural processes that work toward the realization of those ideals. Similar reductions of the meaning of 'God' were carried out in the thirties and early forties of this century by Henry Nelson Weiman and Shailer Matthews at the Divinity School of the University of Chicago, a center of liberal theology in this country. Theological liberalism, Tillich argues, relates Christian message and present situation only at the cost of obliterating the Christian message altogether by reducing it to certain aspects of the present situation.

The last theological movement which Tillich criticizes for failing to fulfill the aim of theology is the *neo-orthodox,* sometimes called *kerygmatic,* theology developed by the Continental theologian Karl Barth. Here Tillich is careful, for he finds many points of affinity between Barth's theology and his own. He praises Barth for his awareness that the eternal truth of the Christian message must not be identified with any finite, temporal expression of it. Part of what Tillich has in mind is Barth's refusal to equate the revelation of God with the words of the Bible. For Barth, God's revelation is experiential, not propositional. (This is a major difference between neo-orthodoxy and fundamentalism.) The words of the Bible, for Barth, record the events of revelation, but are not identical with those events. Consequently, the words of the Bible are finite, human words subject to error. Tillich finds this aspect of Barth's theology commendable, since he sees it as an attempt to get at the Christian message without limiting it to a certain form or set of propositions. He argues, however, that kerygmatic theology fails to relate the Christian message to the present situation. What he refers to is Barth's denial that there is any common ground between theology and philosophy, between Christian message and situation. As Barth puts it, you distort the message if you try to make it reasonable; it is an affront to human reason. "You throw the gospel like a stone." Thus there is no attempt to show how the Christian message constitutes an answer to certain questions which arise out of the situation; there is no attempt to show how divine revelation constitutes a solution to certain philosophical problems about human reason. Tillich argues that the contents of faith should be made plausible to human reason. If the theologian fails to accomplish this, he fails to fulfill one of the basic aims of theology.

If the aim of theology is to relate the eternal truth of the Christian message to the contemporary situation, how is the theologian to proceed in realizing this aim? What sort of method should he employ in developing his theology? It is clear that what Tillich is after is a method in which message and situation can be related in such a way that neither of them is obliterated. He calls the way of proceeding "the method of correlation." About it he remarks:

The following system is an attempt to use the "method of correlation" as a way of uniting message and situation. It tries to correlate the questions implied in the situation with answers implied in the message (ST, 1:8).

In using the method of correlation, systematic theology proceeds in the following way: it makes an analysis of the human situation out of which the existential questions arise, and it demonstrates that the symbols used in the Christian message are the answers to these questions (ST, 1:62).

These two brief remarks, especially the second, are in-structive, for they reveal certain basic convictions under-lying Tillich's vast theological enterprise. These convic-tions may be expressed as follows:

1. There are certain fundamental questions (Tillich calls them existential questions") which arise out of the *situation*.
2. These questions cannot be answered within the situation, even though they arise out of a philosophical analysis of the situation.
3. These questions find their answers in the great symbols in the Christian message.
4. The theologian's task is to interpret the symbols in the Christian message, demonstrating their power to answer the questions that haunt human existence.

But why, we might ask, must this task be undertaken in our time? Is not the human predicament the same for all men at all times? And has not the Christian faith always been proclaimed as the answer to this predicament? If so, why will not some theology from the early Christian or medieval period do for today? To these questions Tillich, I believe, would answer in the following way: First, he would admit, indeed affirm, that there is a universal human predicament to which the Christian message always has been the answer. But he would point out that the way in which man *understands* and *conceptualizes* his predica-ment changes from one period of history to the next. The task of the Christian theologian, therefore, is to *interpret* the Christian beliefs and symbols in terms of the dominant conceptual framework of his own time, showing how the Christian faith answers the 'existential questions' involved in the human predicament. The conceptual framework which Tillich takes to be dominant in our time and in terms of which he analyzes the human situation is derived large-ly, but not entirely, from recent existentialist literature.

Concepts such as *being, essence, existence, estrangement,* and *ambiguity* are employed not only in the analysis of human existence, but also in the interpretation of the Christian symbols. Thus, for example, the symbol of Jesus as the Christ is interpreted, in part, by Tillich as "essential man appearing in a personal life under the conditions of existential estrangement."

As his remarks about the method of correlation indicate, Tillich's program in *Systematic Theology* is (1) to carry out the analysis of the human situation and (2) to interpret the traditional Christian symbols as answers to this situation. The system falls into five parts, each part beginning with a discussion of some aspect of human existence (and existence generally) and ending with the interpretation of a major Christian symbol. These five parts are: Reason and Revelation; Being and God; Existence and the Christ; Life and the Spirit; History and the Kingdom of God.

Thus far I have sought to characterize one of two approaches to Tillich's thought; namely, viewing him as a Christian theologian engaged in writing a theology for the Christian church in our time. But it must be remembered that by training and interest Tillich is also a speculative philosopher. Considering him as such, we may view his work as an attempt to develop a comprehensive interpretation and explanation of man's religious life. It is this view of Tillich that has guided the approach taken and, to a considerable extent, the content included in this book.

Perhaps the most puzzling element that presents itself to the philosopher as he surveys the various forms of man's religious life is the *depth* and *universality* of what we may call the religious attitude. J. N. Findlay has aptly described this attitude as one in which we tend ". . . to abase ourselves before some object, to defer to it wholly, to devote ourselves to it with unquestioning enthusiasm, to bend the knee before it, whether literally or metaphorically."[2] (As we shall see in Chapter I, the religious attitude is what Tillich endeavors to express by his notion of *ultimate concern*.) Religious beliefs, forms of worship, as well as objects of worship vary enormously from one religion to another and within the historical development of each religious tradition. But the religious attitude pervades man's entire religious life. What makes the universal existence of the religious attitude so puzzling is the fact that almost any natural, finite object has been at one time or another the focus of this attitude. Stones, trees, stars, human beings, all have been sacred objects, all have been, in Tillich's terms, the content of ultimate concern. The puzzlement is that a concern of infinite dimensions has been focused on almost any finite object under the sun. Furthermore, in becoming objects of the religious attitude these natural objects become transformed, they take on personal attributes, they become gods. How are we to explain these basic features of man's religious life? How are we to interpret and explain (1) the fact that man is subject to the religious attitude, that he is ultimately concerned, (2) the fact that limited, finite objects become the content of an unlimited concern, and (3) the fact that these objects take on personal attributes and become gods?

One fruitful way of looking at Tillich's philosophical theology is to view it as an attempt to provide a compre-

---

[2] J. N. Findlay, "Can God's Existence Be Disproved," *New Essays in Philosophical Theology,* ed. Antony Flew and Alasdair Macintyre (London: SCM Press Ltd., 1955), p. 49.

hensive explanation of these profound and puzzling religious facts. For this reason, I have focused largely on his doctrine of God and his theory of religious symbols. My purpose, however, is not simply to show how these fundamental elements in Tillich's thought can be viewed as an explanation of the "religious facts" mentioned above. Rather it is to explain and critically evaluate these basic elements themselves.

The first three chapters develop, explain, and examine Tillich's complex doctrine of God. In the last four chapters Tillich's theory of religious symbols is explicated and criticized.

❧1❧

Tillich's Concept of God

PAUL TILLICH'S doctrine of God is at once both religious and philosophical. The religious aspect is expressed by the statement "God is that which concerns man
ultimately" (ST, 1:211). The philosophical aspect of his
doctrine of God is expressed by the statement "God is
being-itself" (ST, 1:235). The task of elucidating Tillich's
concept of God is largely one of explaining these two basic
theistic statements. It is best, I believe, to begin with the
statement "God is that which concerns man ultimately."

The key notion in the statement expressing the religious
aspect of Tillich's doctrine of God is 'ultimate concern.'
Tillich describes ultimate concern as the abstract translation of the great commandment: "The Lord, our God, the
Lord is one; and you shall love the Lord your God with all
your heart, and with all your soul, and with all your mind,
and with all your strength" (ST, 1:11). From this and
other remarks he makes, it would seem that ultimate concern is roughly equivalent to 'utter devotion' or 'complete
commitment.' 'Devotion' or 'commitment' expresses the
element of love mentioned in the commandment. 'Utter' or
'complete' embraces two ideas. First, it means that the

commitment is not divided between God and something else; it is not partial. Second, as expressed in the commandment, the commitment is complete in the sense that all man's dimensions participate in the commitment—the mind, the heart, the soul, etc. Tillich elsewhere expresses this by saying that ultimate concern is a "centered act." "Faith as ultimate concern is an act of the total personality. It happens in the center of the personal life and includes all its dimensions. . . . It is not a movement of a special section or a special function of man's total being. They are all united in the act of faith."[1] Thus to be ultimately concerned about x is to regard x as infinitely important, to be completely committed to x. However, the notion of complete commitment does not quite capture all that Tillich packs into the concept of ultimate concern. To be ultimately concerned about x is not simply to be deeply committed to x; it is also to experience x as *holy*. "What concerns one ultimately becomes holy" (DF, 12–13). What is it to experience or regard x as holy? Refusing to identify holiness with moral perfection, Tillich turns to Rudolf Otto's *The Idea of the Holy*, pointing out that for Otto the awareness of the holy is the awareness of a presence "which remains mysterious in spite of its appearance, and it exercises both an attractive and a repulsive function on those who encounter it" (DF, 13). The holy object is experienced with awe, mystery, dread, and yet one is fascinated by it, irresistibly attracted to it. Tillich contends that these feelings are not peculiar to some one religion, but can be found in

---

[1] Paul Tillich, *Dynamics of Faith* (New York: Harper & Bros., 1957), p. 4. Hereafter references to this work will appear in the text abbreviated as DF.

all religions ". . . because they are the way in which man always encounters the representation of his ultimate concern" (DF, 13). To be ultimately concerned about x, then, is not only to be absolutely committed to x, but to experience x as divine or holy (in the sense explained above). Unless I am mistaken, ultimate concern about x as including absolute commitment to x and certain feelings about x (awe, mystery, etc.), summed up under "experiencing x as holy or divine," is for Tillich a necessary and sufficient condition for x to be a sacred object (religious symbol). I see nothing essentially wrong with this procedure. To identify an object as a religious object is not to identify some property or properties that the object possesses independently of the way in which men react to that object. An object becomes sacred by virtue of becoming the content of ultimate concern.

What must God be for Tillich if He is that about which men are ultimately concerned? The appropriate answer would seem to be "Almost anything." For, given our explication of 'ultimate concern,' it seems reasonable to believe that almost anything could be an object of ultimate concern. At least it is true that human beings and movements (e.g., communism) qualify as objects of ultimate concern. But this creates a difficulty in our attempt to understand what 'God' means for Tillich. For Tillich wishes to equate God with whatever is the object of man's ultimate concern. But, as we shall see, Tillich is not satisfied with a view which ultimately identifies God with a human being or a political movement. This means either (a) Tillich is mistaken in speaking of God as that about which we are ultimately concerned, or (b) he must have a more complex view than I suggested of what it is to be ultimately concerned. The second point b is the more fruitful alternative to explore.

Point b allows several possibilities: (1) Tillich could have a special sense of 'ultimate concern' which is such that one is ultimately concerned *only* about being-itself. The point here is that 'ultimate concern' would be so defined that 'x is ultimately concerned' would *entail* 'x is ultimately concerned about being-itself.' (2) Tillich could be holding that, while we can be ultimately concerned about almost anything, the only satisfactory or appropriate object of ultimate concern is being-itself. If this is his view, then God need not be the only object of ultimate concern. (3) Tillich could be maintaining that ultimate concern—which is defined in terms of certain feelings and attitudes focused on specific objects—is *basically* directed toward being-itself. Point 3 differs from 1 in that it makes the connection between ultimate concern and being-itself a metaphysical connection, rather than an analytic necessity following from a special definition of 'ultimate concern.' It is quite difficult to determine which of these (if any) is Tillich's view. Point 2, more than 1 or 3, fits in best with some of Tillich's statements about idolatry. However, there are passages strongly suggesting 1 or possibly 3:

. . . for that which concerns us ultimately must belong to reality as a whole; it must belong to being. Otherwise we could not encounter it, and it could not concern us. Of course, it cannot be one being among others; then it would not concern us infinitely. It must be the ground of our being, that which determines our being or not-being, the ultimate and unconditional power of being (ST, 1:21).

Here Tillich seems to be denying that we can be ultimately concerned about anything less than the ultimate, being-itself. ('Ground of being,' 'power of being' are both synonymous with 'being-itself' [ST, 1:236].) Anything less than ultimate can be a matter of concern for us, but not of *ultimate* concern. The clearest expression of this point is as follows:

The unconditional concern . . . is the concern about the unconditional. The infinite passion . . . is the passion for the infinite. . . . The ultimate concern is concern about what is experienced as ultimate (DF, 9).

These two quotations seem to make the same general point. We can be ultimately concerned only about what is ultimate, beyond all finite limitations, for only in this way could it have the power of determining our being or non-being. It seems, then, that ultimate concern is a kind of total commitment or complete devotion to the ultimate, being-itself.

But immediately a difficulty emerges. What is it like to be totally committed to being-itself? It may make sense to speak of someone's being totally committed to a person (e.g., Napoleon) or a political movement (e.g., communism), but what sense does it make to speak of someone's being totally committed to being-itself? To clear this up we must explore Tillich's claim that the concrete content of this total commitment (ultimate concern) to being-itself is the religious symbol. In making this point Tillich seems to recognize our quandary over what it could mean to be committed to being-itself.

The phrase "being ultimately concerned" points to a tension in human experience. On the one hand, it is impossible to be concerned about something which cannot be encountered concretely, be it in the realm of reality or in the realm of the imagination. . . . On the other hand, ultimate concern must transcend every preliminary finite and concrete concern. It must transcend the whole realm of finitude in order to be the answer to the question implied in finitude. But in transcending the finite the religious concern loses the concreteness of a being-to-being relationship. It tends to become not only absolute but also abstract, provoking reactions from the concrete element. This is the inescapable inner tension in the idea of God (ST, 1:211).

This means that we must amend our statement that ultimate concern is total commitment to being-itself, the ultimate. For the *focus* of our ultimate concern (total commitment) is something concrete. Without some concrete content we cannot be ultimately concerned. Yet Tillich wants to say also that we cannot be ultimately concerned about what is not the ultimate—and anything that is concrete is not the ultimate. This is beginning to look like a contradiction. Consider these three statements: (1) every concrete thing is less than the ultimate; (2) we can be ultimately concerned only about something concrete; (3) we are ultimately concerned about the ultimate. We cannot assert all three statements without contradiction. Tillich wants to assert something like these three statements, but avoid any contradiction. Let us focus our attention on 2 and 3. I have suggested that the former is necessary if we are to make sense out of ultimate concern as total commitment or complete devotion. To be ultimately concerned is to be totally committed to something. The point here is that the object of total commitment (ultimate concern) must make some demands on us, must be able to promise some sort of fulfillment. In *Dynamics of Faith* Tillich says that that which is our ultimate concern demands total surrender, requires the sacrifice of every other claim to it, promises total fulfillment. It is easy to see how one could love, be devoted and committed to something that can demand total surrender and promise total fulfillment. But what sense does it make to speak of loving, being devoted to being-itself? How does being-itself promise total fulfillment? Napoleon can demand total surrender. Communism can promise total fulfillment. But is it not a mistake to think of being-itself doing these things? Only something concrete can perform these functions and be a direct object of love or devotion. Hence, if we understand ultimate concern as total devotion or complete commitment, we can see the necessity of arguing, as Tillich does, that we can be ultimately concerned only about something concrete.

We must now ask what leads Tillich to the view that we are ultimately concerned about the metaphysical ultimate, being-itself. One possibility, suggested by Alston, is that Tillich is misled by the verbal ambiguity of 'ultimate.' Thus, in his penetrating essay "Tillich's Conception of a Religious Symbol," Alston remarks:

. . . as Tillich explained 'ultimate concern,' the ultimacy is psychological; it consists in the supremacy of that concern in the psychic structure of the individual. It is in a quite different way that being-itself is thought by Tillich to be ultimate. It is ontologically ultimate by virtue of the fact that it is the ultimate ground of all being. Once this distinction is made, we can see that there is no reason to suppose that (psychologically) ultimate concern must be concern directed to what is (ontologically) ultimate. But the verbal identity may make the transition seem obvious.[2]

Alston is certainly correct in pointing out that the *psychological* considerations mentioned in defining ultimate concern do not necessitate that the *metaphysical* ultimate be

2 William P. Alston, "Tillich's Conception of a Religious Symbol," *Religious Experience and Truth*, ed. Sidney Hook (New York: New York University Press, 1961), pp. 20–21.

the object of such concern. If one did think so, he most likely would have been misled by the use of 'ultimate' both for what is psychological and for what is metaphysical. However, it is not clear that Tillich is being misled here, and even if he is he has other reasons for holding that we are ultimately concerned about the metaphysical ultimate. This being so, pointing out that he may be misled by the ambiguity of 'ultimate' will not dispense with his claim unless we also show either that his reasons are not good ones or that they rest on this same ambiguity (which is just a special case of showing that they are not good reasons). Hence, it is necessary to examine the considerations leading Tillich to claim that we are ultimately concerned about being-itself.

A complete account of the considerations which lead Tillich to the view that we are ultimately concerned about being-itself would necessitate a careful discussion of the role of being-itself in his ontology—a discussion that must be left for the next chapter. However, as a preliminary account, we may note the following two claims that Tillich makes: (*a*) we are ultimately concerned about what determines our being or nonbeing—only being-itself can do this; (*b*) we are ultimately concerned about that which can provide an answer to the question implied in finitude— only being-itself can do this since everything else is bound by the conditions of finitude. What *a* and *b* come to, I think, can be set forth in a series of statements.

1. Man is infinitely concerned (anxious) about his being.
2. The source of his anxiety is nonbeing, for nonbeing is what threatens his being.
3. This infinite concern (anxiousness) about his being produces an

infinite quest, longing, for that which can overcome this threat to his being.

4. That which can overcome the threat of nonbeing is being-itself, for only being-itself is not exposed to that threat.

5. Man, therefore, is seeking for being-itself, for some vital contact with that reality which possesses the power of overcoming the existential threat of nonbeing.

6. Since man can encounter being-itself only through the concrete, his infinite quest for being is focused on something concrete through which the power of being is experienced.

Concerning 1, it is important to recognize that by a man's 'being' Tillich does not mean simply his existence in time and space. Rather, when a man is concerned or anxious about his being he is basically concerned about the significance or meaning of his life. Thus Tillich says, ". . . the term 'being' means the whole of human reality, the structure, the meaning, and the aim of existence" (ST, 1:14). The source of this human concern about one's being is, as stated in 2, *nonbeing*. The concept of nonbeing is a fundamental one in Tillich's existentialist ontology of man, as well as in existentialist literature generally. In *The Courage to Be* Tillich endeavors to explain his use of this concept and to suggest the various ways in which nonbeing is experienced as a threat to one's being. Nonbeing, he remarks, threatens our being in three ways:

Nonbeing threatens man's ontic self-affirmation, relatively in terms of fate, absolutely in terms of death. It threatens man's spiritual self-affirmation, relatively in terms of emptiness, absolutely in terms of meaninglessness. It threatens man's moral self-affirmation, relatively in terms of guilt, absolutely in terms of condemnation. The awareness of this threefold threat is anxiety appearing in three forms, that of fate and death (briefly, the anxiety of death), that of emptiness and loss of meaning (briefly, the anxiety of meaninglessness), that of guilt and condemnation (briefly, the anxiety of condemnation). In all three forms anxiety is existential in the sense that it belongs to existence as such and not to an abnormal state of mind as in neurotic (and psychotic) anxiety.[3]

It is not my purpose here to analyze Tillich's concept of nonbeing or to evaluate his claims concerning the ways in which man experiences nonbeing as a threat to his being. My aim is to set forth in logical order the steps by which Tillich comes to the conclusion that being-itself is the object of man's ultimate concern. The first step, as we have seen, is his claim that man is ultimately concerned (anxious) about his own being. The source of this anxiety is nonbeing. The anxiety or concern about one's own being produces in man a quest or longing for that which can overcome the threat of nonbeing, for that which determines our being or nonbeing.

It is important to note that Tillich uses the same expression, 'ultimate concern,' to cover both our *anxiety* concerning our own being and our *longing* for and *commitment* to that which can overcome the threat to our being. Thus he asserts: "Man is ultimately concerned about his being and meaning" (ST, 1:14) and "Man is infinitely concerned about the infinity to which he belongs, from which he is separated, and for which he is longing" (ST, 1:14). It appears, then, that Tillich uses 'ultimate concern' in at least two different senses. Alston draws attention to this ambiguity.

First, "man is ultimately concerned about his being and meaning" in the sense of 'concern' in which it means something like 'being worried about' or 'being anxious about.' ("I am concerned about his

---

[3] Paul Tillich, *The Courage to Be* (New Haven: Yale University Press, 1952), p. 41.

state of health.") But this is a quite different sense from that which Tillich has given to the phrase 'ultimate concern.' Surely Tillich is not suggesting that we are worried about the fate or condition of being-itself![4]

The fact that Tillich uses 'concern' not only in his special sense of 'commitment to,' but also in the more ordinary sense of 'anxious about,' does not in itself signify any error in his reasoning. However, an ambiguity in a crucial expression can easily result in faulty reasoning, for a statement containing the ambiguous expression may be true in one sense of that expression but false in a second sense of that expression. Thus it is important to note the fact that Tillich uses 'ultimate concern' in two different senses. However, I do not think that this particular ambiguity leads Tillich into any serious mistakes.

Tillich holds—for reasons to be investigated later—that being-itself is that which can overcome the threat of nonbeing, for only being-itself is not exposed to that threat. Since man is longing for that which can overcome this threat, Tillich concludes that man is seeking for being-itself, for some vital contact with that reality which possesses the power of overcoming the existential threat of nonbeing. However, since man can encounter being-itself only through the concrete, his infinite quest becomes focused on something concrete through which the power of being is manifested.

The preceding paragraphs represent a brief, general account of the steps by which Tillich is led to claim that man is ultimately concerned about being-itself. However, there is more than one way of picturing the logical progres-

---

[4] Alston, *Religious Experience and Truth,* p. 20.

sion of Tillich's thought in connection with this claim. Instead of taking man's infinite concern about his own being as the starting point, we can just as easily construe Tillich's thought as beginning with a phenomenological description of the relationship of the religious man to some concrete, sacred object. In characterizing the way the religious man experiences and responds to the sacred object, Tillich introduces the concept of *ultimate concern.* 'Ultimate concern' is *defined* in terms of certain human attitudes and feelings focused on sacred objects. Having described what goes on in profound religious experience, Tillich then, quite naturally, seeks to explain why men become ultimately concerned about finite, limited things. Why is it that such a vast variety of finite objects (human beings, animals, statues of stone, etc.) have become objects of man's ultimate concern? Psychological and sociological answers to this question have been given.[5] Tillich, I think, is trying to answer this question in such a way that religion in all its forms is not deprived of objective validity. It is at this point that his elaborate ontology swings into play. Man is striving for that reality which can overcome the threat of nonbeing. Since being-itself is that reality, Tillich concludes that what man is striving for is some vital contact with being-itself. Given this metaphysical background, the phenomenon of ultimate concern focused on sacred objects can be explained as the way in which man's striving for being-itself expresses itself in actual life. Ultimate concern, Tillich concludes, is really directed at being-itself through the concrete, sacred object. Sacred objects,

---

[5] See Tillich's discussion in "The Religious Symbol," *The Journal of Liberal Religion,* 2 (Summer, 1940): 13–33.

then, are the media through which the power of being is communicated to men.

In giving a preliminary account of the considerations which lead Tillich to the view that we are ultimately concerned about the metaphysical ultimate, being-itself, we have distinguished between (1) Tillich's phenomenological description of religious experience and (2) the elaborate ontology he employs in explaining the phenomena of religious experience. In my view Tillich is at his best when he is describing the complex phenomena of religious experience. He has, I think rightly, drawn our attention to the similarities between the attitudes and feelings the "religious man" directs at sacred objects and the attitudes and feelings that men direct at what would normally be regarded as non-religious objects—the state, success, etc. In characterizing these latter attitudes, feelings, and their objects as "religious," as instances of "ultimate concern," Tillich undoubtedly deviates from the common usage of "religion" and "religious." But in so doing he makes us aware of fundamental similarities that our ordinary use of language may conceal. However, it is one thing to describe brilliantly the phenomena of religious experience and to point out the pervasive character of religious attitudes and feelings, and it is quite another thing to endeavor to explain these phenomena in terms of an elaborate metaphysical system involving, as it does, such complicated philosophical concepts as *being-itself, nonbeing, participation,* etc. It is one thing to point out the vast variety of finite objects which have been the focus of religious attitudes (ultimate concern), and quite another thing to explain this phenomenon as the way in which man, in actual life, expresses his ultimate concern about being-itself. For the explanation of the phenomena of religion is given in terms of a particular metaphysics, and the question of the meaningfulness and truth of the metaphysics is not answered by any description, however accurate, of religious experience. In part, the purpose of this book is to single out and critically examine those aspects of Tillich's ontology which bear directly on his doctrine of God. Of chief concern, both in this chapter and the next, is the concept of *being-itself* and the use Tillich makes of this metaphysical concept in developing his doctrine of God.

We began with two statements about God: (1) God is that which concerns us ultimately, and (2) God is being-itself. In exploring 1 it appeared at first that any finite object might be an object of ultimate concern. But a more careful examination of what Tillich says about the situation of ultimate concern disclosed that the finite object is to be understood as the focus of our ultimate concern about being-itself. The finite object *expresses* or *symbolizes* our ultimate concern, which is directed toward the ultimate, being-itself. Hence, 1 and 2 are not incompatible. We must now consider Tillich's assertion that God is being-itself.

Before embarking on the difficult task of determining what Tillich could mean by the expression 'being-itself,' it is necessary to raise the question of the logical status of the statement 'God is being-itself.' Tillich holds that all religious statements about God are *symbolic* (ST, 1:9). Does the statement 'God is being-itself' have the same logical status as religious statements about God? Or is this statement one which Tillich regards as literal? It is not difficult to find an answer to this question in Tillich's writings. The difficulty is to find a consistent answer. For it seems to me that Tillich has shifted his view on this question at least twice in print. If the first two volumes of his *Systematic Theology* were consistent on this question, we could take the answer they give as revealing Tillich's mature opinion on the matter. But, as I shall show, one of the two shifts occurs between volumes 1 and 2 of the *Systematic Theology*. Hence it is necessary to set forth the development of Tillich's thought on this topic and to indicate the shifts that have occurred before we can decide the matter, if we can decide it at all.

In an essay appearing in 1940 in the *Journal of Liberal Religion,* entitled "The Religious Symbol," Tillich made two assertions that drew serious criticism from the pen of Wilbur M. Urban. In his discussion Tillich argued that the distinguishing feature of the religious or mythical symbol is its reference to the transcendent. Urban takes the same position.[6] However, Tillich asserted that the referent of the religious symbol transcends even being. "The thing referred to in the mythical symbol is the unconditioned transcendent, the source of both existence and meaning, which transcends being-in-itself as well as being-for-us."[7] Tillich's critics understood 'being-in-itself' as referring to the metaphysical ultimate. Urban claimed Tillich's view was contradictory. Aubrey expressed the criticism as follows:

Dr. Urban's objection to the phrase applied to the unconditioned—"which transcends being-in-itself"—I share. The idea appears to come from Boehme's *Ungrund* and indicates a negation of all

---

[6] See Wilbur M. Urban, *Language and Reality* (New York: Macmillan, 1939), chap. 12.

[7] Tillich, *Journal of Liberal Religion,* 2 (Summer, 1940): 26.

descriptions. But since the phrase "being-in-itself" is usually employed to connote the ultimate, the notion that there could be that which transcends the ultimate strikes me as a logical impossibility.[8]

In a reply to both Urban and Aubrey published in the *Journal of Liberal Religion* (1940, pp. 202–6), Tillich accepted this criticism and suggested that all he wished to prevent was the identification of God with some special being.

The second, and related point, on which Tillich was criticized by Urban concerned Tillich's assertion that "all knowledge of God has a symbolic character."[9] Tillich's point is that while one can and does experience the unconditioned as the ground and abyss of everything conditioned, there is no positive, literal characterization of the unconditioned that can be given. Hence all our statements about God are necessarily symbolic. Urban characterized Tillich's view as *pan-symbolism*—"the view, namely, that *all* knowledge of God has a symbolic character. As I have sought to point out, the notion of symbolic knowledge (and symbolic truth) is meaningless except in contrast with nonsymbolic knowledge."[10]

Now if we take Urban to be saying that it is meaningless to assert that all statements about God are symbolic (as Tillich apparently understood Urban), I do not think Tillich accepted this criticism in his 1940 reply to Urban and Aubrey. At least he nowhere in the reply suggests that we can make any literal statement about God. But by 1951, with the publication of volume 1 of the *Systematic Theol-*

---

[8] Aubrey, *Journal of Liberal Religion,* 2 (Spring, 1941): 202.

[9] Tillich, *Journal of Liberal Religion,* 2 (Summer, 1940): 28.

[10] Urban, *Journal of Liberal Religion,* 2 (Summer, 1940): 35–36.

ogy, Tillich took the position that there is exactly one statement about God that is literal—the statement that God is being-itself.

> The statement that God is being-itself is a nonsymbolic statement. It does not point beyond itself. It means what it says directly and properly; if we speak of the actuality of God, we first assert that he is not God if he is not being-itself. Other assertions about God can be made theologically only on this basis (ST, 1:239).

That Tillich credits Urban's criticism with showing him the necessity of at least one statement about God being nonsymbolic is clear from the following:

> An early criticism by Professor Urban of Yale forced me to acknowledge that in order to speak of symbolic knowledge one must delimit the symbolic realm by an unsymbolic statement. I was grateful for this criticism, and under its impact I became suspicious of any attempts to make the concept of symbol all-embracing and therefore meaningless. The unsymbolic statement which implies the necessity of religious symbolism is that God is being-itself, and as such beyond the subject-object structure of everything that is.[11]

---

[11] Charles W. Kegley and Robert W. Bretall, eds., *The Theology of Paul Tillich* (New York: Macmillan, 1959), p. 334. In his book, *Paul Tillich and the Christian Message* (New York: Scribner's, 1962), Father Tavard is careless in his quotation of this passage and, as a result, misunderstands what Tillich is saying. He writes: "What then is the unsymbolic statement that makes symbolic knowledge possible? It is 'that God is being-itself and as such beyond the subject-object structure of everything that is.' It is interesting to note that contrary to Tillich's impression, this is a beautiful instance of symbolic language. The word 'beyond' as applied to the Unconditional is obviously a symbol, . . ." (pp. 55–56). But Father Tavard neglects to note that there is a comma between 'being-itself' and 'and' in the statement he quotes from p. 334 of *The Theology of Paul Tillich*— thus giving the impression that the unsymbolic statement is: "God is being-itself and as such beyond the subject-object structure of everything that is." The correct quotation is "that God is being-itself, and as such beyond the subject-object structure of everything that is." This makes it clear that 'beyond' is not part of the unsymbolic statement. The unsymbolic statement is simply "God is being-itself"—this is certainly made clear on p. 239 of *Systematic Theology* 1.

Hence, it seems that one shift Tillich has made is from the position that all statements about God are symbolic to the position of volume 1 of the *Systematic Theology* that there is exactly one statement about God that is nonsymbolic, namely, the statement that God is being-itself.[12]

The second shift in Tillich's thought seems to occur in the Introduction to volume 2 of the *Systematic Theology*.[13] I say "seems to occur" for on the very next page Tillich continues to speak of "defining God as being-itself."[14] Be this as it may, Tillich makes the point in the Introduction that "everything religion has to say about God, including his qualities, action, and manifestation, has a symbolic character . . ." (ST, 2:9). He then raises the question whether there is a point at which a nonsymbolic assertion about God must be made, and says: "There is such a point, namely, the statement that everything we say about God

---

[12] I fail to see the force of Urban's criticism. Apparently he is arguing that 'symbolic' is a *polar* concept and is unintelligible without its polar opposite, 'nonsymbolic' or 'literal.' Hence, to say "all knowledge is symbolic" is senseless because it is an essential feature of the meaning of 'symbolic knowledge' that it be in contrast with 'nonsymbolic knowledge.' The same sort of argument has been given in connection with other pairs of words such as, 'large' and 'small,' 'vague' and 'clear,' 'animate' and 'inanimate' (see N. Malcolm, "Moore and Ordinary Language," in *The Philosophy of G. E. Moore* [Evanston: Northwestern University Press, 1942], pp. 264–65). I do not wish to quarrel with this general point. Nor do I wish to argue that 'symbolic' and 'nonsymbolic' are not instances of this general point. The point which Urban's argument overlooks is that Tillich's original claim is with reference only to God. It is one thing to claim that (1) all statements about God are symbolic, and another thing to claim that (2) all statements about anything whatever are symbolic; 2 may be meaningless, but the fact that 2 is meaningless does not entail, by itself, that 1 is meaningless.

[13] See *Introduction* above, note 1.

[14] This remark assumes that Tillich would count a definition of 'God' as a statement about God.

28

is symbolic. Such a statement is an assertion about God which itself is not symbolic. Otherwise we would fall into a circular argument" (ST, 2:9).

If I understand this passage correctly, Tillich is here implying that 'God is being-itself' is not the straightforward, nonsymbolic statement he took it to be in the first volume. He still holds that not every statement about God can be symbolic. But now he says that the one nonsymbolic assertion about God is the statement, (1) Every statement about God is symbolic (I take 1 to be equivalent to (2) Everything we say about God is symbolic.) If this is so then 'God is being-itself' can no longer be the simple nonsymbolic statement of volume 1. Tillich suggests as much:

If we say that God is the infinite, or the unconditional, or being-itself, we speak rationally and ecstatically at the same time. These terms precisely designate the boundary line at which both the symbolic and the non-symbolic coincide (ST, 2:10).

In fact, once we examine Tillich's new position that (1) Every statement about God is symbolic, it begins to look like the original position that Urban criticized with one small difference—Tillich now wishes to call 1 a statement about God which is nonsymbolic. But is not this addition a mistake? Statement 1 is not a statement about God but a statement about statements about God, namely, that all of them are symbolic. Tillich's original position was that no positive, literal characterization could be given of God as the unconditioned. To give a positive, literal characterization of something is to attach a positive predicate to that thing (e.g., 'loves,' 'created heaven and earth,' 'first cause') and to claim that the resulting assertion is to be taken literally. But to say 'Every statement about God is symbolic' is not to attach a positive predicate to God at all. It is to say something about statements about God. Tillich could reply that even though 1 does not have the same form as a statement like 'God is the first cause' or 'God created heaven and earth'; nevertheless, it does tell us something about God, it does provide some information concerning the unconditioned. What it tells us is that God is *incomprehensible* in the sense that no literal, positive predicate can be meaningfully applied to him. Thus while 1 appears to be about theological statements and not about God, it really is about God since it tells us that he is incomprehensible. But even if this were true, 1 turns out to be just another way of saying that we can give no positive, literal characterization of God—and this is precisely Tillich's original position as set forth in the 1940 essay "The Religious Symbol." Hence 1 implies that the statement 'God is being-itself' must be taken symbolically rather than literally.

I have discussed Tillich's shifts concerning the question of the logical status of the statement 'God is being-itself' since it is of considerable importance in elucidating Tillich's concept of God, to determine whether 'being-itself' applies symbolically *or* literally to God. As we have seen, Tillich's writings do not yield a consistent answer to this question. But before we proceed, some disposition of this question must be made. As far as this study is concerned, the doctrine of volume 1 will be accepted; namely, that 'God is being-itself' is a literal (nonsymbolic) identity statement. This has the consequence that the ontological status of God and the ontological status of being-itself are not two different questions but one and the same question. If being-itself were not identical with God but simply a symbol for God, these two questions would be distinct. I take the doctrine of volume 1 because it is not clear that Tillich means to be denying it in the passages quoted from volume 2. I think the denial is implied, but it is not clear that Tillich is aware of this. I say this is not clear because in restating some aspects of his doctrine of God (set forth in volume 1), Tillich makes a point of saying "in none of these cases has the substance of my earlier thought changed, but formulations have proved to be inadequate in clarity, elaboration, and emphasis" (ST, 2:5). Be this as it may, having accepted as Tillich's position the view expressed in volume 1, we may now proceed with our discussion of the question: What meaning does Tillich attach to the expression 'God'?

The meaning of 'God' is expressed by Tillich in the phrases 'being-itself,' 'the ground of being,' or 'the power of being' (ST, 1:235–36).[15] Of course, this alone will not suffice. The objection to explaining 'God' by these phrases is that the phrases themselves must be explained if we are to discover what 'God' means in Tillich's thought. A second objection is that 'God' is primarily a religious notion, whereas the phrases used in explaining the meaning of 'God' are primarily philosophical. Is there any reason to suppose that in using the former, religious people are referring to what Tillich means by the latter? Even if a

---

[15] However, see Kegley and Bretall, *The Theology of Paul Tillich*, p. 335, where in reply to a criticism by Randall, Tillich rejects the literal equivalence of the phrases and takes the position that 'power' and 'ground' are *symbols* for being-itself.

reply can be given to the first objection—that is, even if we can explicate satisfactorily the notion of being-itself— what grounds does Tillich have for identifying a basically religious notion with a basically philosophical notion?[6] Is the move from the religious level to the philosophical level anything more than arbitrary? I wish to take up both these objections—but in the reverse order in which I have presented them.

It should be noted that, in identifying a philosophical concept (being-itself) and a religious concept (God), Tillich is not doing anything new in theology. Aquinas did substantially the same thing when he argued for the existence of a first efficient cause and then added "to which everyone gives the name of God." We might want to ask in the case of Aquinas whether this is what people actually mean when they use the expression 'God.' Even more, in the case of Tillich, we wonder whether 'being-itself' is what people actually mean when they use the expression 'God.' It is some such puzzlement as this which lies behind the objection to the procedure of telling us what the expression 'God' means by referring us to a philosophical concept such as 'first cause' or 'being-itself.' Perhaps we should say that Tillich, unlike Aquinas, does not claim to be relating his discussion to what 'everyone' means by the expression 'God.' Perhaps he only intends to be telling us what he means by it. But this move does not reflect Tillich's concern to relate his characterization

---

[6] By a religious expression I mean an expression which has a place in religious activity—prayer, worship, reciting creeds, etc. Thus 'being-itself' is not (or, at least, not primarily) a religious expression, whereas 'God' obviously is.

of 'God' to the way in which the expression is used in actual religions. My suggestion is that, in identifying God with being-itself, Tillich is trying to develop a doctrine of God which adequately accounts for what he regards as a basic *tension* in the way in which 'God' is used and God is experienced in actual religions. If we clarify this tension in the actual use of the expression 'God,' we can get some idea of the problem which the notion of being-itself is set up to deal with.

In discussing the meaning of 'God,' Tillich points out:

A phenomenological description of the meaning of "God" in every religion, including the Christian, offers the following definition of the term "god." Gods are beings who transcend the realm of ordinary experience in power and meaning, with whom men have relations which surpass ordinary relations in intensity and significance (ST, 1:211-12).

Tillich proceeds to discuss each element of this description of the meaning of 'God.' It is in this discussion that the tension in the actual use of the expression 'God' becomes clear. The tension Tillich points to is between the "tendency toward concreteness" and the "tendency toward ultimacy." As religious people use the expression 'God,' it refers to a being who exhibits human qualities and limitations. God is influenced by human action and in turn influences human actions. "Gods are substances, caused and causing, active and passive, remembering and anticipating, arising and disappearing in time and space" (ST, 1:212). God is spoken of as located in a burning bush, in a tabernacle, in pieces of bread and drops of wine. All this is very familiar in a religion. It is to these features of the use of the expression 'God' that Tillich is pointing when he speaks of the "tendency toward concreteness" in the idea of God.

But there is also a strong tendency toward ultimacy.

. . . not only do the images of the gods bear all the characteristics of finitude—this makes them images and gives them concreteness —but they also have characteristics in which categorical finitude is radically transcended. Their identity as finite substances is negated by all kinds of substantial transmutations and expansions, in spite of the sameness of their names. Their temporal limitations are overcome; they are called "immortals" in spite of the fact that their appearance and disappearance are presupposed. Their spatial definiteness is negated when they act as multi- or omnipresent, yet they have a special dwelling place with which they are intimately connected. Their subordination to the chain of causes and effects is denied, for overwhelming or absolute power is attributed to them in spite of their dependence on other divine powers and on the influence finite beings have on them (ST, 1:212–13).

Tillich is making two points here. First, he is arguing that there is another tendency in the use of the expression 'God.' Gods are called immortals, invisible, possessors of unlimited power, possessors of perfect knowledge, etc. In speaking of God, religious people deny that he is subject to any empirical limitations, that he is bound by space or time, that there is anything he does not know. God is felt to be mysterious, incomprehensible, absolutely unconditioned. It is to these features that Tillich is pointing when he speaks of the "tendency toward ultimacy" in the idea of God. The second point he is making is that there is a genuine tension or struggle between the two tendencies of ultimacy and concreteness. It can be objected here that not all religious people experience this tension in the decisive way Tillich suggests. Does the mystic refer to God as having a spatial location, dependent on other divine powers, etc.? However, in spite of negative instances, as a general characterization of the idea of God as it occurs in various religions, Tillich's description in terms of a tension between two diverse tendencies is quite acceptable. Of course, a given religion or even a given period in the history of a religion may move in one direction more than another. Consequently, in discussing religions Tillich develops various types ranging from forms of polytheism (emphasis on concreteness) to mystical monotheism (emphasis on ultimacy).

I have suggested that Tillich's identification of God and being-itself is not an arbitrary move but is an attempt to develop a doctrine of God which adequately accounts for a basic tension in the concept of God as it is employed in a religion. This tension refers to our speaking about God both as a concrete being, subject to various limitations and as absolutely transcendent, beyond all limitations. I wish now to make some general remarks concerning the way in which Tillich tries to account for this tension by means of identifying God with being-itself. The rationale for doing this is that it will provide some direction to the task of determining what Tillich means by 'being-itself.'

Tillich's discussion of being-itself moves around two fundamental assertions. The first assertion is that every being is subject to limitations; whereas, being-itself is beyond all limitations. The second assertion is that every being participates in being-itself. Both assertions are made in the following statement:

As the power of being, God transcends every being and also the totality of beings—the world. Being-itself is beyond finitude and infinity; otherwise it would be conditioned by something other than itself, and the real power of being would lie beyond both it and

35

that which conditioned it. Being-itself infinitely transcends every finite being. . . . On the other hand, everything finite participates in being-itself and in its infinity. Otherwise it would not have the power of being. It would be swallowed by nonbeing, or it would never have emerged out of nonbeing (ST, 1:237).

Tillich uses the first assertion to account for the aspect of ultimacy in the idea of God. The argument here is that religious statements about God must be statements about either *a* being or being-itself. But every being is subject to limitations which the tendency toward ultimacy in the idea of God denies. Hence, in developing a doctrine of God, it is a mistake for a theologian to identify God with *a* being. God must be thought of as being-itself, for only being-itself can account adequately for the aspect of ultimacy.

But if being-itself can account for the aspect of ultimacy by virtue of being beyond all limitations, how is Tillich able to accommodate the aspect of concreteness in the idea of God? For if being-itself is free of all limitations, it cannot be concrete. Tillich's solution here is interesting. He appeals to the second assertion about being-itself, namely, that every being participates in being-itself. The argument here is that, by virtue of the participation of every being in being-itself, every being has the potential to express the concrete element in the idea of God. That is, Tillich is arguing that the relationship of participation between being-itself and every being makes it possible for a particular being to become a focal point through which God is disclosed. (Apparently he holds that, in order for a being to mediate or manifest God to man, that being must stand in some *ontological relationship* to God. This is a necessary, but not a sufficient, condition of revelation.)

When any being becomes such a focal point—a sacred object or religious symbol—Tillich views that being as an expression of the tendency toward concreteness in the idea of God. Hence Tillich thinks he can account for the concrete element in religious experience and religious discourse about God by means of the presence and disclosure of the divine in the concrete, made possible by the fact that concrete beings *participate* in being-itself (God).

The preceding paragraphs give rise to two critical questions: First, Can we make any sense out of Tillich's notion of being-itself? Clearly only to the extent that it is possible to do so can we say that Tillich has given an intelligible, let alone adequate, account of the aspect of ultimacy in the idea of God. Second, Does Tillich's theory of religious symbols provide a coherent and adequate account of the concrete element in the idea of God? Although these questions appear to be logically independent of one another, they are not. For, as we shall see, Tillich makes use of the concept of being-itself in the development of his theory of religious symbols. In the rest of this chapter, as well as the next, I shall endeavor to answer the first of these two questions. The second question will be explored in later chapters.

We have seen that the philosophical concept of *being-itself* is introduced by Tillich in order to give an adequate account of certain tensions present in religious discourse about God. This indicates that Tillich takes the view that religious statements about God are to be elucidated, or at least partly explained, by translating them into metaphysical statements—in this case into metaphysical statements about being-itself. However, it should be obvious that the value of the proposed elucidation will depend on the extent to which we can understand what Tillich means by the expression 'being-itself.' Thus in order for us to understand Tillich's use of the concept *God* and his analysis of theological statements (statements with 'God' as the subject expression—e.g., 'God is the creator of heaven and earth') we must be able to give some answer to the question, What is the meaning of 'being-itself'?

What does Tillich mean by 'being-itself'? Rather than give an unclear answer to this question, I propose to raise and answer a prior question; namely, is it possible to answer this question, and, if it is possible, what *kind* of answer can be given? There are at least three ways in which one might try to answer such a question. If one is asked what he means by a certain term, one way in which he can answer is by giving a *definition* of the term in question. However, this way is not open to Tillich. It is impossible to define being-itself, Tillich argues, because it is presupposed in every definition.[17] If one is unable to give a definition of the term in question, he still might be able to provide a more familiar expression equivalent in meaning to the term in question.[18] Tillich does propose 'power of being' and 'ground of being' as substitutes for 'being-itself.' However, there are two reasons why these will not

---

[17] Paul Tillich, *Biblical Religion and the Search for Ultimate Reality* (Chicago: University of Chicago Press, 1955), p. 19.

[18] One might speak of such an expression as a synonymous definition in contrast, say, to definition *per genus et differentia.* If so, then Tillich's claim that it is impossible to define being-itself must not be extended to synonymous definitions, for he seems to hold that there are expressions identical in meaning with being-itself. Thus he says, "Many confusions in the doctrine of God and many apologetic weaknesses could be avoided if God were understood first of all as being-itself or as the ground of being. The power of being is another way of expressing the same thing in a circumscribing phrase" (ST, 1:235–36).

help us here. First, 'power of being' and 'ground of being' are as much in need of elucidation as the original expression, 'being-itself.' If we understood the substitutes it is unlikely that we would have been in the dark concerning the original. Second, when pressed on these matters, Tillich withdraws 'power of being' and 'ground of being' as literal equivalents and suggests that they are symbols for God or being-itself.[19] Hence, these two substitutes will not do as attempts to explain the literal meaning of 'being-itself.' Even if one is prevented from giving a definition or providing an expression which is equivalent in meaning, perhaps he might still give a partial answer by indicating that what he is talking about is of the same general sort as other entities with which we are acquainted. Thus, if one introduces the term 'citrine,' one can indicate what is meant by pointing out that citrine is a *color*—in this way indicating what sort of entity citrine is. Now is this way a possibility for Tillich? I am not sure what the right answer is to this question. It is clear that we cannot say what sort of entity being-itself is if this involves saying that being-itself is an x where 'x' designates a class of beings. The point here is that Tillich holds that *every being* is subject to the structure of being. This implies that of every class of beings it is the case that every member is subject to the structure of being. This case is analogous to saying that since every animal is a living thing, it will be true that of every class of animals—man, canine, etc.—every member is a living thing. Now if we are to say what sort of thing a is by saying a is a man, we cannot deny that a is a living thing. If we deny initially that a is a living thing we can-

---

19 Kegley and Bretall, *The Theology of Paul Tillich*, p. 335.

not say what we mean by 'a' by saying *a* is a man. Similarly, since Tillich holds that only being-itself is not subject to the structure of being, he cannot say what he means by 'being-itself' by saying that being-itself is an *x* where 'x' designates a class of beings.

The real question here is, I think, whether on Tillich's theory, we can literally predicate any general terms of an entity without presupposing that the entity is subject to the structure of being. If we cannot, then there is no way of making a literal positive statement about being-itself. Hence, in saying what Tillich means by being-itself we could choose only what seem to be appropriate metaphorical or symbolic statements. Tillich's position is not clear on this point. Certain remarks he makes suggest that he does hold that no literal statement can be made about being-itself.

As we already have seen, God as being-itself is the ground of the ontological structure of being without being subject to this structure himself. . . . Therefore, if anything beyond this bare assertion is said about God, it no longer is a direct and proper statement, no longer a concept. It is indirect, and it points to something beyond itself. In a word, it is symbolic (ST, 1:239).

Notice that it is because God is being-itself that no positive, literal assertion can be made about him. Much the same point is made concerning the attachment of concepts like *cause* to God or being-itself. For Tillich, to say *x* is a cause in the literal sense of 'cause' is to imply that *x* is a part of the causal series, that *x* is an effect as well as a cause. 'Cause' gets its meaning in application to entities, subject to the structure of being. If we say that God or being-itself is the first cause, this means "that the category of causality is being denied while it is being used. In other words, causality is being used not as a category but as a symbol" (ST, 1:238). Statements such as these suggest that Tillich is holding that general terms and predicate expressions get their meaning by being attached to entities subject to the structure of being. Hence, they cannot be applied *literally* beyond the structure of being. When we do so apply them, they must be taken symbolically, not literally. If this were the case with all our general terms (and Tillich gives us no reason for thinking it is not) then every statement about being-itself would be metaphorical or symbolic. In fact, Tillich says at one point, "Every assertion about being-itself is either metaphorical or symbolic."[20] If this is so, and if 'x is ineffable' is understood as 'no positive, literal assertion can be made about x,' we can say that on Tillich's theory being-itself is *ineffable*.[21]

The main difficulty we have thus far uncovered in trying to explicate Tillich's concept of God can be expressed as follows: (1) to explicate Tillich's concept of God we must first understand what 'being-itself' means; (2) being-itself is ineffable. Two points follow from 1 and 2. First, there is something wrong with Tillich's proposed elucidation of our admittedly analogical or symbolic discourse about God in terms of ontological statements about being-itself. For on his own account being-itself is ineffable and consequently, statements about being-itself must be construed as symbolic or analogical. Thus the ontological statements

---

[20] *The Courage to Be,* p. 179.

[21] There seems to be a difficulty here. Tillich argues elsewhere that "in order to speak of symbolic knowledge one must delimit the symbolic realm by an unsymbolic statement" ("Reply to Interpretation and Criticism," in Kegley and Bretall, *The Theology of Paul Tillich,* p. 334). Now he seems to be saying that no unsymbolic statement can be made about being-itself.

—at least those whose subject term is 'being-itself'—seem as much in need of elucidation as the theological statements they were to elucidate. Second, there does not seem to be any clear answer to the question "What does Tillich mean by 'God'?" For any answer to this question must involve an elucidation of what is ineffable, being-itself. In view of this, the best that can be done, it seems to me, is to compare and contrast the role that *being-itself* plays in Tillich's philosophical theology with the role of ineffable concepts in more fully worked out metaphysical systems. Thus, for example, one can compare and contrast being-itself in Tillich with The Good in Plato and The One in Plotinus. This, of course, will be profitable only if The Good or The One is more intelligible than being-itself and, hence, may serve to illuminate the latter. This, it seems to me, is the direction in which one must proceed if he hopes to get a philosophically adequate interpretation of Tillich's concept of God, if such an interpretation is possible. It is in this direction that we shall proceed.

❧II❧

Models for Interpreting Being-Itself

I HAVE argued both that any elucidation of Tillich's concept of God must involve an elucidation of the ontological notion *being-itself*, and that the most promising
way of proceeding with the latter is by way of comparing
and contrasting the role that being-itself plays in Tillich's
philosophical theology with the role of similar concepts in
more fully worked out metaphysical systems. Of course,
any of a number of philosophical concepts might be
examined as possible models for interpreting Tillich's concept of being-itself—for example, Plato's the Good, Plotinus' concept of the One, Spinoza's notion of substance, and
Kant's concept of the thing-in-itself. The procedure fol-
lowed here is to employ the concept of a *universal* and
Plotinus' concept of the *One* as models for illuminating
Tillich's concept of being-itself. To be more precise I shall
select certain features often ascribed to universals and suggest that certain remarks Tillich makes about being-itself
become intelligible if we construe being-itself as possessing something like these features. The same procedure will
be adopted in comparing the One and being-itself.

The first task is to explain, at least in part, what I mean to be saying about x when I say x is a universal. In what follows I will assume that we are able to distinguish certain entities as universals and certain other entities as particulars. That is, given entities such as John, Fido, justice, and charity, I shall assume that we know that the first two are particulars and that the last two are universals. Secondly, in what follows I make no claim to be setting forth a set of criteria which will effectively distinguish universals and particulars. Various attempts can be made to distinguish them: (1) universals, unlike particulars, are not in space; (2) universals, unlike particulars, are not temporally located; (3) universals are predicable, particulars are not; (4) universals, not particulars, can be exemplified; (5) universals, not particulars, can characterize another entity; (6) universals are said to be eternal, but not particulars. Doubtless, there are difficulties with these attempts to distinguish universals from particulars. For example, consider the claim that universals, unlike particulars, are not in space. One difficulty here is that entities that we would normally count as particulars (e.g., a particular mental image) are not said to be *in space*. However, in spite of such difficulties, I shall select from these attempts to distinguish universals from particulars certain features which I intend to be ascribing to x when I say that x is a universal. That these features may not be adequate to distinguish anything we would want to call a universal from anything we would want to call a particular is not a matter of great importance for my purpose. What is important is that (1) the features I suggest are exhibited by many entities Tillich and the philosophic tradition would call universals and (2) these features, when applied to *being-itself*, may illuminate certain remarks Tillich makes concerning being-itself.

The first feature which x possesses if x is a universal is that it is predicable. The second feature that x possesses if x is a universal is that x is neither spatially nor temporally located. These two features are, I think, exhibited by the entities which philosophers have traditionally regarded as universals—justice, charity, humanity, treehood, etc. When I say that x is a universal I mean to be saying both that x is predicable and that x is neither spatially nor temporally located. A third and final feature I mean to ascribe to anything I speak of as a universal is that it has extra-mental existence. This third feature is associated with a particular philosophical theory regarding the ontological status of universals; namely *realism* (extreme and moderate). I include it here because I believe that Tillich stands in the realist tradition regarding universals and because I think that if we adopt this view we can better understand some of the remarks Tillich makes about being-itself.

I have said that universals are predicable. Suppose A asserts, 'Socrates is wise.' The universal *wisdom* is here predicated of Socrates. The reason for saying this is that when asked what it is that he is predicating of Socrates, A can appropriately reply, 'Wisdom.' Notice that the response to the question, 'What is it that is being predicated of Socrates?' is different from the natural response to the question 'What is it that is asserted of Socrates?' or to the question, 'What is it that Socrates is asserted to be?' *Wisdom* is what is predicated, *that he is wise* is what is asserted of Socrates, and *wise* is what Socrates is asserted to be. Thus we are led to say that universals are predicable because a universal is the appropriate answer to the question 'What is predicated of x?'

There is a close connection between the view that universals are predicable and certain other attempts, 4 and 5, to state the difference between universals and particulars. The questions 'What is Socrates said to exemplify?' and 'What is it that is said to characterize Socrates?' can also be answered by 'wisdom.' Universals are predicable of things, they characterize things, they are exemplified by things. The things of which they can be predicated are either particulars or universals. Socrates is a particular and wisdom is a universal. In 'Socrates is wise' and 'Wisdom is a virtue' we are predicating wisdom of Socrates and virtue, or being a virtue, of wisdom. Traditionally, it has been held that while universals can be predicated of universals or particulars, particulars cannot be predicated at all. In 'The teacher of Plato is Socrates' we are not predicating Socrates of the teacher of Plato but identifying the two.

I have said that universals are neither spatially nor temporally located. What is usually said is that the particular instances or exemplifications of a universal—a wise man, a man, a tree—are subject to spatial and temporal location. But the universals—wisdom, humanity, treehood, etc.—are not.

Finally, I indicated that when I say x is a universal I mean to be saying that x has extra-mental existence or reality. A universal is not a mental idea. This I take to be a crucial point in the realist's theory of universals. When we take this third feature in conjunction with the first, we obtain the consequent that whenever we say 'x is a man' or 'x is a tree' or 'x is wise' we presuppose the reality or existence of manhood, treehood, or wisdom. I will refer back to this point since it may serve to illuminate Tillich's claim that the reality of being-itself is presupposed whenever anything is said to be. At least, I think we can see how one would be led to make that claim if being-itself is understood as possessing something like the features I am ascribing to universals.

I have introduced the concept of a universal into this discussion in order to throw some light on certain statements Tillich makes and certain questions he asks about being-itself. The task now is to see if these statements and questions become intelligible if we construe being-itself as possessing some of the features I have ascribed to universals.[1] We can begin, where Tillich does, with a question. "What is being-itself? What is that which is not a special being or a group of beings, not something concrete or something abstract, but rather something which is always thought implicitly, and sometimes explicitly, if something is said to *be*" (ST, 1:163)? It is instructive to note that this question is basically similar in form to a question we might ask about a universal.[2] For example, "What is humanity-itself? What is that which is not a special human being or a group of humans, but rather something which is always thought implicitly, and sometimes explicitly, if something is said to be human?" The similarity of these two questions suggests that being-itself may be similar in some respects to humanity-itself. That is, it suggests that

---

[1] The close connection between Tillich's concept of *being-itself* and the traditional concept of a *universal* has been noted and discussed by Sydney Hook in *The Quest for Being* (New York: St. Martin's Press, 1961), pp. 157–58. Thus on p. 157 he remarks: ". . . Tillich is using the term Being as if it were an essence or universal, and his employment of the word 'participates' suggests that he is treating it as a platonic essence or universal."

[2] This similarity was pointed out by Hook. See Hook, *The Quest for Being*, p. 157.

being is regarded as predicated of every being in the way in which we may regard *humanity* as predicated of every man. If this suggestion is correct, then just as we might analyze 'John is a human being' as the predication of a universal (humanity) of a particular (John), so Tillich would regard 'John is a being' or 'John *is*' as the predication of *being* of a particular (John). At any rate if we construe being as *predicable* in the way a universal is predicable I think we can understand why Tillich should ask the question he does and why he should claim that being-itself is somehow implied whenever anything is said to *be*.

Construing being-itself as possessing the features I ascribed to universals also may illuminate one of the fundamental statements Tillich makes about being-itself. As I pointed out earlier, Tillich asserts that every being participates in being-itself. In the philosophic tradition 'participation' has been used to designate the relation of particulars to entities characterized by the features I have ascribed to universals. Particulars are said 'to participate' in universals. Men participate in humanity. Likewise, every being participates in being-itself. What I am suggesting is that if we construe being-itself as possessing the three features I have ascribed to universals we can understand at least why Tillich says "every being participates in being-itself." A stronger case for construing being-itself in this way could be made if it were clear that Tillich uses 'participation' in this context to designate a relation similar to the relation between particulars and universals. Unfortunately, Tillich never says what he means by 'participation' in "Every being participates in being-itself." Furthermore, he does indicate that 'participation' is used in several different ways.

The concept of participation has many functions. A symbol participates in the reality it symbolizes; the knower participates in the known; the lover participates in the beloved; the existent participates in the essences which make it what it is under the conditions of existence; the individual participates in the destiny of separation and guilt; the Christian participates in the New Being as it is manifest in Jesus the Christ (ST, 1:177).

Can we say which of these uses, if any, Tillich has in mind when he says that every being participates in being-itself? Some of these uses can be excluded. The participation of every being in being-itself cannot be that of symbol to reality symbolized because, as we shall see later, not every being is a symbol of being-itself (although every being has the potentiality to become a symbol). The participation in question cannot be that of knower to known since not every being can be a knower. The last two uses of participation—the individual in the destiny of separation and guilt, and the Christian in the New Being—can be ruled out on the grounds that not every being (i.e., existing thing) is an 'individual' (the sense in question here seems to involve being a *person*) or a 'Christian.' This leaves one sense of 'participation': "the existent participates in the essences which make it what it is under the conditions of existence." It is by participating in *being* that something *is, exists.* It is by participating in *humanity* that something *is human.* 'Participation' in this context seems to designate the relation between particulars and universals. Hence, it would seem that by 'participates' in "Every being participates in being-itself" Tillich means to designate a relation not unlike the relation said to hold between particulars and universals. If so, then it is plausible to construe being-itself as possessing something like the three features I have ascribed to universals.

A third point which is partially illuminated by construing being-itself in the way I have suggested involves the conjunction of two statements: (*a*) universals are 'powers of being,' and (*b*) being-itself is 'the power of being.' I mentioned earlier that Tillich holds a realist position with regard to universals. In distinguishing an essence or universal from an existing thing Tillich points out that the universal has being but does not exist. The thing that exists (in this case a tree) "stands out and exists only because it participates in that power of being which is treehood, that power which makes every tree a tree and nothing else" (ST, 2:21). Here Tillich explicitly speaks of a universal, *treehood,* as a *power of being.* He regards universals as powers of being, "the powers of being which make a thing what it is" (ST, 1:254). Thus Tillich holds *a,* the first part of the conjunction noted above. That Tillich holds *b* is clear from the following. "Ever since the time of Plato it has been known—although it often has been disregarded, especially by the nominalists and their modern followers—that the concept of being as being, or being-itself, points to the power inherent in everything, the power of resisting nonbeing" (ST, 1:236). Given Tillich's characterization of universals as powers of being and given the interpretation of being-itself as possessing certain basic features ascribed to universals, it is not unnatural that Tillich should speak of being-itself as the power of being.

A fourth point made by Tillich that is illuminated by the interpretation of being-itself we have been considering is his claim that God can be conceived *properly* only if he is conceived as being-itself. The reason why he holds this is that to conceive God as *a* being rather than being-itself involves a contradiction. What Tillich is arguing is that the conception of God as the being *par excellence,* the highest, most perfect being, is a contradiction. If this is so, and if God must be conceived as unlimited, unconditioned, then we must conceive of God as being-itself if we are to conceive him at all. The problem here is to see why Tillich thinks that the conception of God as the infinite, unconditioned being is contradictory. The problem is to see what leads him to say: "Whenever infinite or unconditional power and meaning are attributed to the highest being, it has ceased to be *a* being and has become being-itself" (ST, 1:235). My suggestion is that this claim is both intelligible and plausible if being-itself is construed as possessing the features I have ascribed to universals. However, it is necessary here to say something about universals which I have not explicitly said before. The relation of a particular to a universal in which it participates is a *dependence* relation. We can express this by saying x is ϕ only if (1) there is ϕ-ness and (2) x participates in ϕ-ness. ϕ-ness is a precondition for x being ϕ. Now let us suppose that being-itself is in this respect like a universal and that the relation of *a* being to being-itself is similar to the relation of x to ϕ-ness. If so, I think we can see why Tillich regards an *infinite, unconditioned being* as contradictory. For by virtue of being a being, it is *ipso facto* dependent for its existence on being-itself. It is conditioned by and subordinate to being-itself just as a tree is conditioned by and subordinate to treehood. A tree is limited, conditioned by the nature of treehood and a being is limited, conditioned by the nature of being-itself. This is why if (1) God must be conceived as unconditioned and (2) every being is conditioned by the structure or nature of being-itself, (3) God must be conceived as being-itself. Either God is being-itself or a being (the highest being). But if God is a being (even the highest being) he still would be *subordinate* to being-itself; hence, he would not be unconditioned. "A theology which does not dare to identify God and the power of being as the first step toward a doctrine of God relapses into monarchic monotheism, for if God is not being-itself, he is subordinate to it, just as Zeus is subordinate to fate in Greek religion" (ST, 1:236).

In the foregoing I have suggested that if being-itself is construed as possessing certain features ascribed to universals there are at least four claims Tillich makes concerning being-itself that are illuminated in the sense that we can partially understand the claims and why Tillich should make them. The four claims I have discussed are: (1) being-itself is presupposed (thought explicitly or implicitly) whenever anything is said to *be*, (2) every being participates in being-itself, (3) universals are "powers of being" and being-itself is "the power of being," and (4) God can be conceived properly only as being-itself for every being, even the highest being, is conditioned by being-itself. By using the concept of a universal as a model we have been able to interpret these claims about being-itself and give some explanation as to why Tillich should make them. But it is one thing to elucidate these claims by ascribing to being-itself certain features often ascribed to universals, and quite another thing to *identify* being-itself with a universal, even the highest universal. That the latter would be a misleading, if not false, account of Tillich's concept can be brought out by raising the question of the *existence* of universals and being-itself.

One significant consequence of *identifying* being-itself with a universal is that the existence of God (being-itself) becomes entangled with the question of the existence of universals. Any disproof of the existence of universals would be a disproof of the existence of God. This suggests that any attempt to establish the ontological validity of Christianity would have to take into account the arguments advanced by nominalists against the claim that universals exist. That is, it would have to be admitted that if the nominalist position is correct God does not exist. Hence, one way of deepening our understanding of Tillich's concept of being-itself is to examine what he has to say about nominalism, its attack on universals, and what he takes to be the implications of this attack for his concept of being-itself.

Tillich does believe that nominalism is false. He rests his claim on the following argument:

> According to nominalism, only the individual has ontological reality; universals are verbal signs which point to similarities between individual things. Knowledge, therefore, is not participation. It is an external act of grasping and controlling things. Controlling knowledge is the epistemological expression of a nominalistic ontology; empiricism and positivism are its logical consequences. But pure nominalism is untenable. Even the empiricist must acknowledge that everything approachable by knowledge must have the structure of "being knowable." And this structure includes by definition a mutual participation of the knower and the known. Radical nominalism is unable to make the process of knowledge understandable (ST, 1:177).

It is difficult to follow the line of reasoning Tillich pursues in this argument. Apparently, he thinks nominalism entails the claim that knowledge is not participation. He then argues that the assertion 'knowledge is not participation' is false. Hence, nominalism is false. Three questions have to be asked about the argument: (1) What does Tillich mean by the assertion 'knowledge is not participation'? (2) In what way does nominalism entail that assertion? (3) Why is that assertion false? If we knew what Tillich means by 'participation' perhaps we could answer 1. But, as I have already indicated, Tillich uses 'participation' in many different ways—although he fails to explain on any given occasion of its use just what he means by it. I suspect that the answer to 1 must be given along the following lines. To claim that knowledge is participation is to claim that there *is* some universal shared by both the knower and the known, it is to claim that some universal exists and characterizes both knower and object known. If this is involved in the answer to 1, it is clear why nominalism contends that knowledge is not participation. For by virtue of its claim that universals are merely *verbal signs* nominalism contends that there *are* no universals shared by both knower and known. That is, nominalism asserts that only individuals exist, universals do not exist. Thus nominalism must assert that knowledge is not participation. But why is the assertion 'knowledge is not participation' false? The reasoning here is curious. Everyone, Tillich argues, must admit that the objects we know have the structure of "being knowable." To deny this, presumably, is to deny that we can have any knowledge of those objects. But the fact that objects of knowledge have this structure of being knowable implies, by definition, that there *is* some universal possessed by both knower and known. Hence, nominalism is untenable—at least once we admit that we have knowledge of any object.

The argument, then, is a particular version of the general claim that we cannot give an intelligible account of the nature of knowledge if we deny the existence of universals. I am not concerned with arguing that Tillich's version of this claim is true or that it is false. The point of introducing the argument was to show *that* and *why* Tillich thinks nominalism is false. However, even though Tillich believes nominalism is false, it will be helpful to consider what he says about the nominalist's criticism of universals and why he thinks that the criticism does not apply to being-itself.

The criticism of the nominalists and their positivistic descendants to the present day is based on the assumption that the concept of being represents the highest possible abstraction. It is understood as the genus to which all other genera are subordinated with respect to universality and with respect to the degree of abstraction. If this were the way in which the concept of being is reached, nominalism could interpret it as it interprets all universals, namely, as communicative notions which point to particulars but have no reality of their own. Only the completely particular, the thing here and now, has reality. Universals are means of communication without any power of being. Being as such, therefore, does not designate anything real. God, if he exists, exists as a particular and could be called the most individual of all beings.

The answer to this argument is that the concept of being does not have the character that nominalism attributed to it. It is not the highest abstraction, although it demands the ability of radical abstraction. It is the expression of the experience of being over against non-being. Therefore, it can be described as the power of being which resists non-being. For this reason, the medieval philosophers called being the basic *transcendentale*, beyond the universal and the particular. In this sense the notion of being was understood alike by such people as Parmenides in Greece and Shankara in India. In this sense its significance has been rediscovered by contemporary existentialists, such as Heidegger and Marcel. This idea of being lies beyond the conflict of nominalism and realism. The same word, the emptiest of all concepts when taken as an abstraction, becomes the most meaningful of all concepts when it is understood as the power of being in everything that has being (ST, 2:10–11).

The nominalist argues that general concepts such as 'humanity' and 'being' do not designate anything real; only particulars are real. Tillich wishes to avoid the nominalist's conclusion that 'being' does not designate anything real.

Two avenues are open. First, Tillich can argue that nominalism is in fact false. We already have examined one argument Tillich uses to show that pure nominalism is false. But the argument did not show that the nominalist's thesis was incorrect with regard to 'being.' The second avenue is to show that the nominalist's criticism does not apply to 'being' and, consequently, to the question of the reality of God. It is this approach that Tillich now takes.

It is, undoubtedly, clear by now that in giving an answer to the nominalist Tillich cannot say, as many theologians would not hesitate to say, that the criticism is inapplicable because God is a particular being (the highest being) and not a universal. Tillich consistently refuses to consider God as *a* being, as a particular being. Hence, what he must do is distinguish 'being' from the concepts to which the nominalist criticism is applicable.

Tillich's argument has two steps. First, he points out that the nominalist's criticism makes the assumption that the concept of being is a genus to which all other genera are subordinate in two respects: (1) universality—they are less universal than *being* and (2) abstractness—they are less abstract than *being*. Tillich admits that if this were the way he arrived at the concept of being—that is, if 'being' were arrived at by abstracting what is common in concepts less universal than itself—then nominalism could proceed to deny the existence of God (being-itself) in the same way in which it denies all other universals. The second step in the argument is Tillich's claim that the concept of being is not the most abstract concept, the most universal genus attained by a process of abstraction—hence, the basic assumption nominalism makes is false. And, since (1) this assumption is entailed by the criticism and (2) this assumption is false, it follows that (3) the criticism of nominalism is inapplicable to 'being' and, consequently, to the question of the reality of God. Our task is to understand why the assumption the nominalist makes about the concept 'being' is false.

The assumption is that 'being' is the highest genus both in universality and abstractness. In the passage quoted, Tillich gives two reasons why this assumption is false. First, he makes the *negative claim,* that 'being' is *not* the highest abstraction. Secondly, he makes the *positive claim* that 'being' designates the power of being in everything that has being—"The same word, the emptiest of all concepts when taken as an abstraction, becomes the most meaningful of all concepts when it is understood as the power of being in everything that has being" (ST, 2:11).

Tillich argues that 'being' is not the highest genus or the highest abstraction. The point he is making was made by Aristotle. Aristotle argues that the species of every genus are distinguished from one another by differentia which do not fall under that genus. Consider, for example, the concept 'animal.' This is a universal concept, it is applicable to a number of particulars: *a* is an animal, *b* is an animal, *c* is an animal. Furthermore, the concept 'animal' marks out a genus. There are species which subdivide 'animal'—for example, 'man,' 'horse,' 'canine'—and 'animal' is determinable into its species by the addition of differentia which lie *outside* the concept 'animal.' Thus the species 'man' is determined by the addition of 'rational' which lies outside the genus 'animal.' Aristotle says, ". . . it is not possible for the genus taken apart from its species (any more than for the species of the genus) to be predicated of its proper differentia; so that if unity or being is a genus, no differentia will either have being or be one."[3] What this means is that if 'being' is a genus, then the differentia of the species of being must *not* have being. But this is impossible; hence, being cannot be a genus. "But it is not possible that either unity or being should be a single genus of things; for the differentia of any genus must each of them both have being and be one, . . ."[4]

My interest here is not to determine whether Tillich is correct in saying that the nominalist's attack makes the assumption that being is the highest genus in universality and abstractness. My purpose is to illuminate Tillich's concept of being or being-itself. And it is important to note that Tillich does not consider 'being' as an abstract universal, a concept arrived at by abstracting what is common in concepts less universal than itself. If we think of universals as arrived at by a process of abstraction, it is clear that we cannot interpret Tillich's concept of being or being-itself as a universal. The relation between the concept 'being' and the concepts denoting various kinds of being is not the same as the relation between the concept 'animal' and the concepts denoting various kinds of animal.

The positive claim Tillich makes is that 'being' designates the power of being in everything that has being. He says that the concept of being is not the highest abstraction but "is the expression of the experience of being over against non-being" (ST, 2:11). He then says that this is why the medieval philosophers called being the basic *transcendental,* that Parmenides, Shankara, Heidegger, and Marcel all understand *being* as the power of being

---

3 Aristotle *Metaphysics* 3. 3. 998b23-27.

4 *Ibid.* 3. 3. 998b21-23.

which resists nonbeing. The line of argument is difficult to follow in this passage. For one thing it is unclear whether Tillich means to be accepting the medieval view of 'being' as a transcendental term. A transcendental term is like a universal in that it is a *predicate*. However, it is distinguished from universals on at least two counts: (1) it is predicated of everything and (2) it is predicated of different things analogically, rather than univocally. I say it is unclear that Tillich accepts this view of 'being' because in the passage under consideration he appears to be asserting as his own view that 'being' designates the power of being in everything that has being. He then says that this is *why* the medieval philosophers called being the basic transcendental. Now, it is true, I think, that Tillich regards 'being' as universally predicable. But does he hold that it is predicated analogically, rather than univocally? To my knowledge Tillich neither asks nor answers this question. It could be argued, however, that he is logically committed to this view, for he has already admitted that we do not arrive at the concept 'being' by the process of abstraction by which we arrive at the concept 'animal' or the concept 'living thing.' The latter are attained by abstracting what is common from the differences of various species. Thus the differences are neglected. But we cannot arrive at the concept 'being' in this way owing to the fact that the differences also share in being. In the case of 'animal' or 'living thing' the universal concept does not "actually contain the differences of its inferiors." This, clearly, is not true of 'being.' The differences of its inferiors are actually contained in being. Having agreed to this, the question is whether Tillich can avoid the view that being is predicated analogically, rather than univocally. Coffey, for example, gives the view already accepted by Tillich as *the reason* why 'being' is not predicated univocally of beings.

A generic concept can be predicated *univocally*, i.e., in the same sense, of its subordinate species. These latter differ from one another by characteristics which lie outside the concept of the genus, while they all agree in realizing the generic concept itself; they do not of course realize it in the same way, but as such it is really and truly in each of them and is predicated in the same sense of each. But the characteristics which differentiate all genera and species from one another, and from the common notion of being, in which they all agree, are likewise *being*. That in which they differ is being, as well as that in which they agree. *Hence we do not predicate "being" univocally of its various modes.* When we say of the various classes of things which make up our experience that they are "real" (or "realities," or "beings"), we do not apply this predicate in altogether the same sense to the several classes; for as applied to each class it connotes the whole content of each, not merely the part in which this agrees with, but also the part in which it differs from, the others.[5]

Whether or not Tillich would accept Coffey's argument is a matter of speculation. Hence, we cannot determine whether Tillich's concept of 'being' shares one of the basic features that many medievals ascribed to 'being' and other transcendental terms. That is, we cannot determine whether Tillich would distinguish 'being' from 'universals' in the sense of holding that the former can only be predicated analogically of various beings while the latter can be predicated univocally of the entities falling under them. However, in spite of this indeterminacy, there are at least two respects in which we can say that Tillich construes 'being' as many medievals construed it and other transcendental terms. First, Tillich holds that 'being' does not mark out a genus, that 'being' is not arrived at by abstracting

---

[5] P. Coffey, *Ontology* (London: Longmans, Green and Co., 1914), p. 36.

only what is common in the various kinds of being. Secondly, Tillich seems to agree that 'being' is predicated of everything. This suffices to show that it would be a mistake to identify being with a universal, even the highest universal, so long as we think of a universal as *abstract* in the sense developed above.

Our discussion so far has been aimed at elucidating the concept of being-itself in Tillich's philosophical theology. We saw how several basic remarks he makes about being-itself become intelligible if we ascribe to being-itself certain features often ascribed to universals. I then raised the question whether it would be correct to *identify* being-itself with a universal, perhaps the highest universal. By examining Tillich's discussion of nominalism we saw that such an identification would be a mistake if we understand a universal as containing only what is common among the different entities characterized by the universal. There is, however, a more profound reason why it would be a mistake to rest too heavily on the notion of a universal or essence as an adequate model for interpreting being-itself. While the model is helpful in interpreting certain remarks Tillich makes about being-itself, it directly conflicts with Tillich's explicit claim that *God is beyond essence and existence* (ST, 1:236).

Clearly, if God is beyond essence and existence it is as serious a mistake to identify God with an essence or universal as it is to identify God with an existing being. Concerning the latter identification, we noted earlier that if God were *a* being he would, on Tillich's ontology, be dependent on being-itself. This is impossible since it is analytic that God does not depend on anything. However, it is also clear that if God were identified with *a* being, we could not say, as Tillich does, that God is *beyond* existence. Similarly, if God were identified with an essence or universal, we could not say, as Tillich does, that God is *beyond* essence. Tillich, of course, recognizes this; hence, after adopting the view that God is beyond essence and existence, he argues:

> For this reason it is as wrong to speak of God as the universal essence as it is to speak of him as existing. If God is understood as universal essence, as the form of all forms, he is identified with the unity and totality of finite potentialities; but he has ceased to be the power of the ground in all of them, and therefore he has ceased to transcend them (ST, 1:236).

Having explored the concept of a universal as a possible model for interpreting Tillich's concept of being-itself, we may now turn to a discussion of what is perhaps a more fruitful model—Plotinus' concept of the One.

In his attempt to give a metaphysical account of the nature of things, Plotinus invokes three explanatory principles: the One, *Nous,* and Soul (*Ennead* 5:1). For our purposes, we need consider only the One and its relation to *Nous* and other beings. *Nous* or the Divine Mind is a real being, the first offspring of the One. The Divine Mind knows itself and in knowing itself knows the essence of all actual and possible things. From *Nous* proceeds Soul and from the latter proceeds the material world. Having postulated the Divine Mind and having indicated how Soul and the material world are to be understood as proceeding from it, the question arises for Plotinus as to why it is necessary to postulate the One as prior to the Divine Mind. It is his answer to this question and the philosophical consequences of his answer that may provide a basis for illuminating certain aspects of being-itself that we have been unable to account for up to this point.

A fundamental premise in Plotinus' answer is that every duality or plurality presupposes a unity from which it can be derived. He sometimes says that what is complex must proceed from something more simple. He then argues that the Intellectual Principle (*Nous,* the Divine Mind) involves a duality, and concludes that it must proceed from absolute unity (the One). "In the first place, Plurality is later than Unity. The Intellectual Principle is a number (= the expression of a plurality); and number derives from unity: the source of a number such as this must be the authentically One" (*Ennead* 3:8, 9).[6] His reason for saying that the Divine Mind involves duality is that it knows itself. That is, there is a duality in the Divine Mind of knower and known, even though in this case the knower and the known are identical. He says of *Nous,* "It is the sum of an Intellectual-Being with the object of its Intellection, so that it is a duality; and, given this duality, we must find what exists before it" (*Ennead* 3:8, 9). We must now see what Plotinus says about that which comes 'before' *Nous.*

That which precedes *Nous* cannot be either the knower or the intelligible object (the known) for these two are involved in an inseparable duality. What then can it be? "Our answer can only be: the source of both" (*Ennead* 3:8, 9). That which precedes *Nous* is the source of *Nous.* But, asks Plotinus, "What will This be; under what character can we picture it?" Perhaps we can describe it as "The Good" and "the wholly simplex." If we do so describe it

---

[6] Quotations are from the translation by Stephen MacKenna.

Plotinus allows that we will not be in error, "but we will not be giving any certain and lucid account of it as long as we have in mind no entity in which to lodge the conception by which we define it" (*Ennead* 3:8, 9). The point seems to be that in order to successfully ascribe a property to that which precedes *Nous* we must have some knowledge of what *it* is to which we are ascribing the property. Plotinus then points out that we can have no literal, descriptive knowledge of that which is the source of *Nous*. For, "our knowledge of everything else comes by way of our intelligence; our power is that of knowing the intelligible by means of the intelligence: but this Entity transcends all of the intellectual nature; . . ." (*Ennead* 3:8, 9).[7] How then can we even speak of it? Plotinus answers, "We indicate it by virtue of what in ourselves is like it. For in us, also, there is something of that Being; nay, nothing, ripe for that participation, can be void of it" (*Ennead* 3:8, 9).[8] However, so long as we speak of literal, descriptive knowledge, Plotinus is insistent that no such knowledge can be gained of being-itself. Of course, we can assert *literal*, negative propositions about that which is the source of everything but we can have no positive, literal knowledge of it. Plotinus makes this clear in a passage which parallels much that Tillich says of being-itself.

-----

[7] A similar point is in Tillich. Our descriptive knowledge involves the subject-object structure, the basic structure of being. Being-itself, however, transcends the structure of being.

[8] Tillich argues in a similar fashion. The only knowledge we can have of God or being-itself is symbolic or analogical knowledge. No literal knowledge can be had because God transcends the structure of being. Symbolic knowledge is possible because everything participates in being-itself (ST, 1: 239–40).

The Unity, then, is not Intellectual-Principle but something higher still: Intellectual-Principle is still a being but that First is not being but precedent to all Being: it cannot be a being for a being has what we may call the shape of its reality but the Unity is without shape, even shape Intellectual. Generative of all, The Unity is none of all; neither thing nor quantity nor quality nor intellect nor soul; not in motion, not at rest, not in place, not in time; it is the self-defined, unique in form or, better, formless, existing before Form was, or Movement or Rest, all of which are attachments of Being and make Being the manifold it is.

But how, if not in movement, can it be otherwise than at rest? The answer is that movement and rest are states pertaining to Being, which necessarily has one or the other of both. Besides, anything at rest must be so in virtue of Rest as something distinct: Unity at rest becomes the ground of an attribute and at once ceases to be a simplex. Note, similarly, that when we speak of this First as Cause we are affirming something happening not to it but to us, the fact that we take from this Self-enclosed: strictly we should put neither a This nor a That to it; we hover, as it were, about it, seeking the statement of an experience of our own, sometimes nearing this Reality, sometimes baffled by the enigma in which it dwells (*Ennead,* 6, 9, 3).

Even his name for it, *the One,* cannot be taken in any literal sense. Plotinus is clear that it is not 'one' in a mathematical sense, i.e., one as the first of a series, or as the monad and point are the one reached by a division of what is many (*Ennead,* 6:9, 6). "It is not one in any sense in which oneness can be predicated of anything else, nor is its oneness a predicate of itself. In a word, it is only in a negative sense as a denial of plurality, and by analogy, that we apply the term."[9]

At this point we may well ask what distinguishes Plotinus' *One* from absolutely nothing at all. For we can argue, paralleling Plotinus, that it is a mistake to think of *nothing*

---

[9] B. A. G. Fuller, *The Problem of Evil in Plotinus* (Cambridge: Cambridge University Press, 1912), p. 58. Also see, William R. Inge, *The Philosophy of Plotinus,* 2 (London: Longmans, Green, and Co., 1919), 108.

as being either at rest or in motion, that it is a mistake to think of *nothing* as *a* being, as complex, as either ignorant or knowing, as a this or a that. It seems that anything we might select to distinguish the One (or, for that matter, Tillich's being-itself) from nothing at all is found to be a property the possessor of which is *a thing*, and, since the One is not a thing, that property cannot be used to distinguish the One from nothing. Plotinus, I think, would reply to this objection by insisting that we do know something about the One which distinguishes it from nothing. We know that it is the source, the ground, of all that exists, apart from it there would indeed be no *things* at all. Hence, he insists: "We know it as a cause of existence to Intellectual-Principle, as fount of all that is best, as the efficacy which, self-perduring and undiminishing, generates all beings and is not to be counted among these its derivatives to all of which it must be prior" (*Ennead* 6:9, 5). As to how that which is no thing can generate all things, Plotinus is uncertain, but that in some way it does he is certain. If it did not exist, nothing at all would exist; if it did not generate, nothing but it would be. After rejecting various attempts to describe it, he asks, "And what will such a Principle essentially be?" His answer is:

The potentiality of the Universe: the potentiality whose non-existence would mean the non-existence of all the Universe and even of the Intellectual-Principle which is the primal Life and all Life. This principle on the thither side of Life is the cause of Life—for that Manifestation of Life which is the Universe of things is not the First Activity; it is itself poured forth, so to speak, like water from a spring. Imagine a spring that has no source outside itself; it gives itself to all the rivers, yet is never exhausted by what they take, but remains always integrally as it was; the tides that proceed from it are at one within it before they run their several ways, yet all, in some sense, know beforehand down what channels they will pour their streams (*Ennead,* 3:8, 10).

So long as Plotinus insists that, however metaphorically or analogically, we can and must say of the One that it is the source of everything that exists, it is clear that no matter how much is denied of it, the One is distinguishable from absolutely nothing.[10] Indeed, as Inge suggests, there are three basic themes about the One that Plotinus inherits from Plato's view concerning the Good. "Three ideas are here inseparable: (1) the Good is the supreme object of all desire and aspiration. (2) the Good is the condition of knowledge; it is that which makes the world intelligible. (3) the Good is the creative and sustaining cause of the world."[11] Despite the fact that the One is beyond all division, beyond the subject-object structure of experience, beyond the literal application of every property that is the property of some *thing,* Plotinus would distinguish the One from nothing by affirming of it the three claims Inge suggests Plato makes about the Good.[12] This completes my brief account of Plotinus' conception of the One. We must now see the extent to which the One illuminates certain quite basic features of Tillich's notion of being-itself.

A consideration of the doctrine that God or being-itself

---

[10] This assumes that Plotinus' basic assertion does not contradict any of the many negative statements he makes about the One. A case might be made that his conception of the One is incoherent for precisely that reason.

[11] Inge, *The Philosophy of Plotinus,* 2:125.

[12] Compare the following passage: "The Good is that on which all else depends, toward which all existences aspire as their source and their need, while Itself is without need, sufficient to Itself, aspiring to no other, the measure and Term of all, giving out from itself the Intellectual-Principle and Existence and Soul and Life and all Intellective-Act" (*Ennead,* 1: 8, 2).

transcends the distinction between essence and existence disclosed that: (1) God cannot be identified with a universal or essence, even the highest essence and (2) God cannot be conceived as *a* being, even the highest being. The model of a universal was found to be inadequate as a way of illuminating 1. However, the One, which clearly is neither an essence nor *a* being, does, if we assimilate being-itself to it, help us understand why Tillich should assert 1 as explicity and strongly, if not as frequently, as he asserts 2. The model of the One also can account for Tillich's assertion of 2. Second, in so far as the nominalist's attack assumes that 'being' is arrived at by a process of abstraction, that *being* is a genus, it is clear, modeling being-itself after the One, why Tillich should regard the nominalist's criticism as ineffective against and irrelevant to his conception of being-itself. Third, it would seem that the four claims which we earlier accounted for by ascribing to being-itself certain features often ascribed to universals also can be accounted for by assimilating being-itself to Plotinus' One. Finally, (and this, I regard as perhaps the chief merit of the present comparison) two of the three basic positive remarks Plotinus is prepared to assert (analogically) of the One coincide with, and may help to illuminate, two fundamental remarks Tillich asserts about God (being-itself); namely, (1) God is the supreme object of all desire and aspiration and (2) God is the creative and sustaining ground of everything that exists.

That being-itself is held by Tillich to be the creative and sustaining ground of everything that exists needs no justification at this point. That being-itself is held by Tillich to be the supreme object of all desire and aspiration is implied by Tillich's claim, discussed in Chapter I, that man longs for some vital contact with being-itself. I am not claiming here that either of these basic assertions Tillich makes becomes lucid and clear once we assimilate being-itself to Plotinus' One; for this would be to claim that it is abundantly clear why Plotinus makes the corresponding assertions about the One—and the latter, of course, is not that clear. This is the inevitable drawback of trying to explain the doctrines of one speculative metaphysician by reference to the views of another. It is hoped, however, that the comparison does throw some light on Tillich's notion of being-itself, if only to link it to the tradition of neo-Platonism and the systematic attempt of a well-known philosopher, Plotinus, to give an account of his own basic metaphysical concept—'the One.'

There are, then, (to present something of a summary of the foregoing discussion) at least *six* basic claims Tillich makes about being-itself which (hopefully) are illuminated if we assimilate being-itself to the One. (1) Being-itself is not an essence or universal—it "transcends the distinction between essence and existence." (2) Being-itself is not *a* being. (3) We can have no positive, literal knowledge of being-itself—"every assertion about being-itself is either metaphorical or symbolic." (4) Everything participates in being-itself and depends upon it for its existence—it is the source or ground of everything that is. (5) Being-itself is the ultimate object of all desire and aspiration—"ultimate concern is concern for the ultimate." (6) Being-itself is absolutely unconditioned, beyond any distinction or division.

Unlike the concept of a universal, it is difficult to single out any very fundamental respects by which to distinguish Plotinus' concept of the One from Tillich's concept of being-itself. This may be due, in part, to the fact that neither notion is very precise in itself; hence, it is naturally difficult to find particular points by which to distinguish them. For example, one might think that the One can be distinguished from being-itself by the fact that the One gives rise to the world by a process of *emanation* which is *intrinsic* to the One; whereas, the world does not emanate from God (being-itself) but is freely created by him. However, when Tillich's discussion of "God as creating" is carefully examined it becomes difficult to drive a sharp wedge between what he says and what Plotinus says about the necessary emanation of the world from the One.[13]

However, in spite of the fundamental similarity between these two conceptions of the metaphysical ultimate and the natural difficulty of sharply distinguishing them, I will suggest one respect in which the One does not seem to coincide with Tillich's concept of being-itself. In spite of his professed monism and his recognition of the fact of evil, Plotinus is quite certain that the One is *entirely Good,* that no evil or negative principle can be associated with the One or the process of emanation which gives rise to the world. That is, the One and the process of emanation cannot be thought to contain any evil or negative principle. In fact, Plotinus sometimes speaks of "the Good" rather than "the One." In his account of evil he insists that it has no intrinsic connection with the One, the Intellectual-Principle, or the Soul. "Such is the untroubled, the blissful, the life of

---

[13] See ST, 1:252 ff., and B. A. G. Fuller's discussion of the theory of emanation in *The Problem of Evil in Plotinus,* pp. 229–333. It is clear from Tillich's account that creation is an *eternal process* and that it is intrinsic to God. "The divine life and the divine creativity are not different" (ST, 1:252).

divine beings, and Evil has no place in it; if this were all, there would be no Evil but Good only, the first, the second and the third Good. All thus far, is with the King of All, unfailing cause of Good and Beauty and controller of all; and what is Good in the second degree depends upon the Second-Principle and tertiary Good upon the Third" (*Ennead*, 1:8, 2).[14] Thus Plotinus sharply dissociates negativity and evil from the One.

Tillich, however, seems to take the position that negativity (nonbeing) must be posited in being-itself (God). This is a fundamental aspect of his concept of being, since without nonbeing no thing could *be*. This is so because every thing necessarily participates both in being and in nonbeing. Nonbeing *is*, it is not absolutely nothing. Hence, Tillich thinks that being-itself in some way must contain a principle of negativity. Thus he says:

> If God is called the living God, if he is the ground of the creative processes of life, if history has significance for him, if there is no negative principle in addition to him which could account for evil and sin, how can one avoid positing a dialectical negativity in God himself? Such questions have forced theologians to relate non-being dialectically to being-itself and consequently to God (ST, 1:188–189).

Perhaps then, we can distinguish Plotinus' conception of the ultimate from Tillich's conception in that Plotinus seems to deny that there is any negative principle intrinsic to the One, whereas as we have seen, Tillich posits a principle of negativity within the divine (being-itself). This

---

[14] Passages such as this one suggest a dualistic treatment wherein evil is finally accounted for by some eternal principle (e.g., matter) which is independent of the Good. For a discussion of the dualistic elements in Plotinus' basically monistic position see Fuller's chapter "Matter as the Principle of Evil" in *The Problem of Evil in Plotinus.*

point may explain why Tillich does not employ "the Good" as a substitute for "being-itself."

In both this chapter and the last I have been occupied with the task of explicating Tillich's concept of God. In view of his identification of God and being-itself and his general tendency to explicate the theological statements about God in terms of ontological statements about being-itself, it became necessary to discuss the notion of being-itself. Although being-itself is *ineffable* in Tillich's system, I have sought, in the present chapter, to elucidate Tillich's remarks about being-itself by comparison and contrast with the concept of a universal and Plotinus' concept of the One. It will further our understanding of Tillich's concept of God—as well as disclose certain difficulties in that concept—if we now turn to an examination of what he has to say about the existence of God.

❧III❧

The Existence of God

PERHAPS the most disturbing feature of Tillich's philosophical theology is his claim "God does not exist" (ST, 1: 205). Is Tillich then an atheist? But how can a Christian theologian be an atheist? These questions come to mind when one considers Tillich's rather extraordinary claim.[1] In this chapter I shall (1) endeavor to elucidate Tillich's claim that God does not exist, (2) develop and examine Tillich's reasons for making this claim and (3) raise certain questions about the extent to which this claim can be coherently maintained within his theological system.

Traditionally theologians have sought to present considerations in support of the statement "God exists." These considerations have varied from appeals to direct religious experience to the philosophical arguments of natural theology. However, if we ask what Tillich has to say in support of the existence of God, it would appear that within the framework of his theology we are not raising a sensible question; for, instead of trying to establish the existence of God, he seems bent on denying it.

---

[1] "Is Tillich an Atheist?" was a symposium topic at the meeting of the Western Division of the American Philosophical Association in May, 1960.

It would be a great victory for Christian apologetics if the words "God" and "existence" were very definitely separated. . . . God does not exist. He is being-itself beyond essence and existence. Therefore to argue that God exists is to deny him (ST, 1:205).

Thus the question of the existence of God can be neither asked nor answered. If asked, it is a question about that which by its very nature is above existence, and therefore the answer—whether negative or affirmative—implicitly denies the nature of God. It is as atheistic to affirm the existence of God as it is to deny it (ST, 1:237).

Consider the two statements: "God exists" and "God does not exist." The second passage quoted suggests that Tillich is not saying simply that the first of these statements is false, and the second true. This way of putting it would be misleading. He regards both assertions as mistaken. Both assertions are atheistic, blasphemous in Tillich's view, for both suggest that God is the sort of entity that *could* exist. And it is this view that Tillich thinks is mistaken. Perhaps Tillich's point can be put in this way. Consider sentences of the form 'x does not have φ.' The contexts in which such sentences are most frequently used are those where it is *conceivable* that x should have φ. It is this possibility that makes the assertion significant and informative. For example, 'Jones does not have red hair,' 'Brown does not have a college degree.' However, in extraordinary circumstances one might use a sentence of the form 'x does not have φ' where it is *inconceivable* that x should have φ—for example, 'The number two is not red.' The number two is not the sort of thing that could be red. Thus we can distinguish two different contexts in which a negative assertion can be made: (1) 'x does not have φ' where it is *conceivable* that x should have φ, and (2) 'x does not have φ' where it is *inconceivable* that x should have φ. When Tillich says "God does not exist" (as in the passage quoted) *he* regards it as an assertion *analogous* to type 2—that is, God is not the sort of entity that conceivably could exist.[2] Since for most it is regarded as a statement analogous to type 1, Tillich thinks that the statement, when so regarded, is as mistaken as the assertion that God exists. "God exists" and "God does not exist" (type 1) are both atheistic on Tillich's view, for they deny the true nature of God. This same point is behind his claim that "the question of the existence of God can be neither asked nor answered." For to ask "Does God exist?" normally presupposes that God is the sort of entity that conceivably could exist. Since Tillich denies the presupposition, he is unwilling to allow the question.

We have seen that when Tillich says "God does not exist" he does *not* mean that it is conceivable that God should exist but as a matter of fact does not. What he means is that it is *inconceivable* that God should exist, that God is not the sort of entity that *could* exist. Of course, this does not mean that for Tillich "God exists" is on a par with "A round square exists." It is inconceivable that a round square should exist; but it is inconceivable because the concept *round* is incompatible with the concept *square*. For Tillich, it is inconceivable that God should exist not because of a contradiction in the concept *God* but because the very notion of existence is incompatible with the nature of God.

Tillich argues: "However it is defined, 'the existence of God' contradicts the idea of a creative ground of essence and existence. The ground of being cannot be found within the totality of beings, nor can the ground of essence and existence participate in the tensions and disruptions char-

---

[2] I stress 'analogous' so as *not* to imply that Tillich regards 'existence' as a substitution-instance for ϕ, a variable ranging over properties.

acteristic of the transition from essence to existence" (ST, 1: 204–5). There are really two reasons given here why the notion of 'existence' is incompatible with the nature of God. The first reason is that God cannot be found in the totality of beings, God is not *a* being. The second reason is that God does not participate in the disruptions of existence.

The main point in Tillich's second reason can be expressed in the following way: 'x exists' implies that x is subject to the conditions of finitude—time, space, causality, and substance. I have made the point in a more general way than Tillich. He speaks of the 'disruptions' characteristic of the realm of existence; whereas I mentioned the conditions of finitude. In his system anything subject to the 'disruptions' of existence is also subject to the conditions of finitude. But the converse need not be true. Christ is the counter-example. Although subject to finitude, he was not caught in the 'disruptions' of existence. But given what Tillich and classical theology say about God, it is clear that God is not subject to the conditions of finitude. Hence, it follows that it is a logical mistake to say that God exists. I do not wish here to take up a discussion of Tillich's analysis of the realm of existence. It is enough to note that he does use 'exists' in such a way that to say 'x exists' is to imply that x is subject to the conditions of finitude. What this means is that 'existence' and 'exists' are *technical* terms in Tillich's system. When people argue about the existence of God they are not arguing about whether God is finite or not. When the classical theologians asserted the existence of God they did not mean to imply, nor were they taken to imply, that God is subject to the conditions of finitude—time, space, etc. Hence, it would seem that Tillich has not given any convincing reason as yet why it would be a mistake to say that God *exists* when 'exists' is used not in Tillich's special sense, but either in its ordinary sense or in the sense in which the classical theologians used it.

To put this criticism of Tillich in another way, we could *give* Tillich the words 'existence' and 'exists' and still raise the question whether God *is*, whether there *is* a God—using 'is' as roughly equivalent to 'exists' in its ordinary, non-Tillichian sense.

Tillich's first reason for denying the existence of God is that God cannot be found within the totality of beings. Given that to be a member of "the totality of beings" is to be *a* being, Tillich's point here is that God does not exist because (1) God is not *a* being and (2) anything that exists is *a* being. The problem is to see what leads Tillich to hold 1 and 2. It is, of course, relevant to point out that for Tillich there is a distinction between *a* being and being-itself, that *a* being is dependent for its existence on being-itself (which alone is independent), and that since God cannot be dependent on anything he cannot be *a* being. This distinction between *a* being and being-itself helps us to understand why Tillich holds 1, but it throws no light on 2. Moreover, it fails to relate 1 and 2 to the discussion of God in classical theology—and I do not think we can understand 1 and 2 apart from some discussion of the conception of God in classical theology. My suggestion is that we must have some understanding of the traditional view that in God there is no distinction between *essence* and *existence* before we can understand what Tillich has to say about the traditional view, how he uses the expression '*a* being,' and why he holds 1 and 2.

Tillich cites classical theology, and Thomas Aquinas in particular, as holding the view that God is beyond essence and existence (ST, 1:236). Thomas draws a distinction between the essence of a thing and its existence. Roughly, this distinction corresponds to the distinction we would draw between *what* a thing is and the fact *that* it is. To say *what* a thing is is to state the *essence* of a thing, that which is signified by the definition of a thing.[3] 'Existence' refers to the act by which an essence has being. "Existence denotes a kind of actuality; since a thing is said to exist, not through being in potentiality, but through being in act."[4]

Copleston points out that the distinction between essence and existence is not a distinction between two separable things but a metaphysical distinction within a thing.

Essence and existence are not two things. There is no objective essence without existence, and there is no existence which is not the existence of something. When Aquinas talks about existence being 'received' or 'limited' by essence (cf. *De ente et essentia*, 6), he does not mean that there is a kind of general existence which is divided up, as it were, among individual things. Inasmuch as existence is always, as far as our experience goes, the existence of some essence, of some particular kind of thing, it can be said to be 'limited' by essence; for it is always the existence of a man or of a horse or of a dog or of some other substance. And inasmuch as the substance considered as essence, is that which has being, that of which we say that it exists, it can be said to 'receive' existence. But these ways of speaking are not meant to imply either that existence is something apart from an essence or that an essence has objective reality apart from existence. The distinction between them is a distinction within a concrete finite being.[5]

---

[3] *Concerning Being and Essence*, ch. 2. I am indebted to Copleston's book on Aquinas (cited below) for this brief interpretation of essence and existence in Thomas.

[4] *Summa Contra Gentiles*, I, 22.

[5] F. C. Copleston, *Aquinas* (London: Penguin, 1955), p. 97.

Having drawn this metaphysical distinction between the essence and existence of a thing, Thomas denies that the distinction applies to God. In God there is no distinction between essence and existence, they are one and the same, God's *essence* is simply *to be*.[6]

As Thomas Aquinas understands him, God is the being whose whole nature it is to be such an existential act. This is the reason why his most proper name is, HE IS. After saying this, any addition would be a subtraction. To say that God "is this," or that he "is that," would be to restrict his being to the essences of what "this" and "that" are. God "is," absolutely. . . . He prefers to say that the essence of God is his *esse*. In other words, God is the being of which it can be said that what in other beings is their essence, is in it what we call "to be."[7]

God, then, for Aquinas, as Tillich points out, is beyond the distinction between essence and existence. Tillich shares this view with Thomas (ST, 1:236).[8] We must now see what Tillich thinks is implied by this conception of God.

We noted earlier that in Tillich's system, if God were *a* being he would be dependent on being-itself. This is impossible since it is analytic—both for Tillich and classical theology—that God does not depend on anything. The difficulty with this piece of reasoning is that the notion of 'a being' is left unclear. If Tillich explicates it in the way in which he does 'exists'—that is, if he holds that to be *a* being, even the highest being, is to be subject to the conditions of finitude—then his position is open to the same

---

[6] *Summa Theologica*, I, Q3, Art. 4.

[7] Etienne Gilson, *History of Christian Philosophy in the Middle Ages* (New York: Random House, 1955), pp. 368–69.

[8] This, of course, assumes that Tillich means roughly what Thomas means by 'essence' and 'existence' and the distinction between the two. While there are significant differences—e.g., Tillich seems to regard the transition from essence to existence as a *fall*—there are enough similarities to merit the assumption here.

criticism that I directed against his view of 'existence.' The virtue of the essence-existence distinction is that we can give a sense to 'a being' apart from any entailment of finitude. That is, x is a being if, and only if, x has an essence distinct from its act of existence. To say that x is a being is to imply that x has an essence which distinguishes x from other species of things and from existence as such. But if, as Aquinas holds, God's essence is identical with his act of existing, if his nature is simply *to be*, there is nothing to distinguish God from existence as such. *His esse* is no other than *esse*. Thus if 'x is a being' implies that there is a distinction between the essence and existence of x, it is not difficult to see why Tillich should hold that *God is not a being*. For, consistent with classical theology, Tillich holds that in God there is no distinction between essence and existence. Furthermore, Tillich may be holding, with good reason, that whenever we assert the existence of x we imply a distinction between essence of x, *what x is*, and the existence of x, *that x is*. If so, then it follows that if x exists then x is a being. Hence, we can see why Tillich would assert that *anything that exists is a being*.

My suggestion is that Tillich's claims may rest on a three-way equivalence of 'x exists,' 'x is a being,' and 'x has an essence distinct from its act of existing.' Assuming this to be so, it is clear that since in God there is no distinction between essence and existence, God cannot be said to *exist* or to be *a* being. On this view the *core* of Tillich's objection to talking about the *existence* of God is that such talk involves making God into *a* being and, thereby, implying a distinction between essence and existence in God. This is a very forceful objection since it is extremely difficult to conceive how one can meaningfully assert that x exists without implying or presupposing a distinction between what x is and the fact that x is.

Thus Tillich thinks that Aquinas has fallen into error in asserting the existence of God, for, as we have seen, Aquinas denies any distinction between essence and existence in God. "The scholastics were right when they asserted that in God there is no difference between essence and existence. But they perverted their insight when in spite of this assertion they spoke of the existence of God and tried to argue in favor of it" (ST, 1: 205).

I indicated that Tillich and Aquinas share the view that God is beyond the distinction between essence and existence. Nevertheless, Aquinas asserts the existence of God, whereas Tillich rejects the application of the concept of existence to God. Perhaps their respective views can be made clear in terms of the following statements:

1. God is beyond *the distinction* between essence and existence.
2. God is beyond essence and existence.
3. In God essence and existence are identical.
4. 'x exists' entails 'x has an essence distinct from its act of existence.'

1 is understood to be compatible with, indeed, entailed by, both 2 and 3. Points 2 and 3 are incompatible, as are 3 and 4. Both Aquinas and Tillich hold point 1. Tillich holds 2, but not 3; whereas, Aquinas holds 3 but not 2. Tillich alone holds 4. What is at issue between them appears to be the proper analysis of the concepts of *essence* and *existence*. Tillich's analysis of these concepts leads him to assert point 4. Holding 4 and 1 he must reject the application of the concept existence to God. Aquinas' analysis of these concepts leads him *either* to reject 4 altogether—

for the reason that God exists but has no essence *distinct* from his act of existence—*or* to hold that 4 is true only of the literal use of these concepts—'essence' and 'existence' being applied to God *analogically.*

The issue between Tillich and Aquinas is too complex to resolve here—nor is it my purpose to try to resolve it. My purpose has been to elucidate Tillich's claim that God does not exist and, more importantly, to explain as fully as possible Tillich's reasons for making that claim. The main suggestion I have made is that his fundamental reason is derived from the classical notions of essence and existence and the distinction between them. In the course of exploring this suggestion I have compared and contrasted Tillich's view with that of Aquinas. I wish now to raise certain questions about the extent to which Tillich's claim, that God does not exist, can be coherently maintained within his theological system.

The paradox in Tillich is that in spite of his claim that existence is incompatible with the nature of God, he nevertheless talks about God in such a way as to imply or presuppose that God exists. It should be obvious that he cannot have it both ways. In the following paragraphs I shall try to show that Tillich implies not only that God exists but that he necessarily exists.

Consider the following statements about God.[9]

1. God transcends the world (ST, 1:237).
2. Every finite thing participates in God (ST, 1:237).
3. God cannot have a beginning and an end (ST, 1:189).
4. Non-being is literally nothing except in relation to God (ST, 1:189).

---

[9] Some of these statements are made about being-itself. But since Tillich identifies God and being-itself (ST, 1: 239), the statements may be regarded as about God.

5. God precedes non-being in ontological validity (ST, 1:189).
6. God is his own beginning and end, the initial power of everything that is (ST, 1:189).

It is odd, to say the least, that all these statements should
be regarded as *true* even though the statement 'There *is*
a God' is held to be false or meaningless. How can it be
true, for example, that every finite thing depends on God
for its existence, if it is not true that there *is* a God on
which every finite thing depends for its existence? Surely
this is no less mystifying than the classical view that God
exists even though in God there is no distinction between
essence and existence. It will not do for Tillich to say
simply that points 1 through 6 are analogical or symbolic.
It needs to be shown that points 1 through 6 can be true
analogical statements about God even though 'God exists'
is false or meaningless—and Tillich has not shown this.
The fundamental difficulty in Tillich on this score is that
he wants both to talk of God (being-itself) in such a way
as to suggest that he exists, but at the same time to preclude the semantic possibility of raising the question of
the existence of God (being-itself). This is convenient for
Tillich since he can talk of God in such a way as to suggest
not only that he *is* but *necessarily* is without having to
defend his position since he precludes the possibility of
significantly denying what he implicitly asserts.

I have suggested that Tillich implies not only that God
(being-itself) exists but necessarily exists. Perhaps the
best way to begin supporting this suggestion is by examining the following statement:

The ontological question, the question of being-itself, arises in something like a "metaphysical shock"—the shock of possible non-being.
This shock often has been expressed in the question, "Why is there

something; why not nothing?" But in this form the question is meaningless, for every possible answer would be subject to the same
question in an infinite regression. Thought must start with being;
it cannot go behind it, as the form of the question itself shows. If
one asks why there *is* not nothing, one attributes being even to
nothing. Thought is based on being, and it cannot leave this basis;
but thought can imagine the negation of everything that *is*, and it
can describe the nature and structure of being which give everything that is the power of resisting non-being (ST, 1:163–164).

Tillich, like many contemporary philosophers, argues that
there is something seriously wrong with the question,
"Why is there something; why not nothing?" In this passage he presents what I think are two distinct reasons for
rejecting this question. The first reason is simply that it is
impossible to answer the question—for whatever *thing* we
refer to in our explanation of why something exists will be
such that the very same question can be asked about it.
To endeavor to answer this question is to initiate an infinite regress of question and answer. For this reason—
namely, that it is impossible to answer the question—Tillich concludes that the question is *meaningless*.

It is doubtful, I think, that the reason Tillich mentions
really justifies the conclusion that the question, "Why is
there something; why not nothing?" is meaningless. For
in the first place, it is not at all clear that his reason is
correct—that is, it is not at all clear that the question cannot be answered. Indeed, the notion of a *necessary being*
—a being whose nature entails its existence, a being that
does exist and logically could not fail to exist—is precisely
what, for many advocates of the cosmological argument,
answers the question.[10] Of course, it may be objected that

---

[10] See, for example, Samuel Clarke's famous discussion of the cosmological argument in his *A Demonstration of the Being and Attributes of
God* (1705).

the idea of a necessary being is itself a confused idea. But the large body of controversial literature on the cosmological and ontological arguments indicates that it is no simple and obvious matter to show that it is confused or meaningless. However, even if we admit that Tillich's reason is, in itself, correct—that is, even if we admit that the question, "Why is there something; why not nothing?" cannot be answered—it does not seem to follow that the question is, therefore, *meaningless.* It may be inappropriate to ask the question, it may be an extraordinary question—since most questions can be answered—but are we justified in concluding that the question is nonsensical, meaningless? Clearly, we are justified only if the following principle (or some principle entailing it) is true; namely, every meaningful question is such that a satisfactory answer to it is possible. Neither Tillich, nor anyone else for that matter, has demonstrated the truth of this principle. Hence, it is doubtful that Tillich's reason provides a sufficient justification for the conclusion that the question, "Why is there something; why not nothing?" is meaningless.

Tillich's second reason for rejecting the question is contained in his remark: "If one asks why there *is* not nothing, one attributes being even to nothing." What he seems to mean is that the possibility that one endeavors to envisage when one asks "Why is there not nothing?"—namely, that "Nothing exists" or "Nothing is"—is not a possibility at all. It is not a possibility because to assert "Nothing exists" or "Nothing is" is to attribute being even to nothing, to predicate existence of what does not exist (i.e., nothing). Hence, the question must be rejected because it asks why something is not so—namely, that nothing exists—which could not conceivably be so. It could not conceivably be so because it involves the contradiction of predicating existence of non-existence (nothing).

I shall later endeavor to show that Tillich is mistaken in assuming that in asking "Why there *is* not nothing?" one attributes being even to nothing. But, for the moment, I want to indicate the role that this assumption plays in what I take to be an argument (in the passage quoted) for the conclusion that God (being, being-itself) necessarily exists. There are, it seems to me, two steps to the argument. (1) We can conceive the non-existence of every being—"Thought can imagine the negation of everything that *is*." The question this point leaves open is whether we can conceive the non-existence of being-itself. (2) We cannot conceive the non-existence of being-itself. This follows from Tillich's statement, "Thought must start with being; it cannot go behind it, . . . If one asks why there *is* not nothing, one attributes being even to nothing." Tillich's point here seems to be that even though it is conceivable that no being should exist, it is inconceivable that nothing should be. For as we have just seen, to assert "Nothing exists" or "Nothing is" is to attribute being even to nothing, to predicate existence of non-existence. Now, given that "Nothing exists" is necessarily false *we* would normally conclude that "Something exists" is necessarily true. However, we cannot do this, given Tillich's refusal to consider being-itself as a possible member of the scope of expressions like 'something' and 'everything' because *thing* denotes, for him, only conditioned, limited entities. The situation seems to be as follows. Every conditioned entity can be conceived as not existing. "Nothing exists" is a contradiction. Hence, "some unconditioned entity exists" must be necessarily true. Being-itself is the unconditioned entity. Hence, "being-itself exists" is necessarily true.

Tillich's view that God (being-itself) necessarily exists is reminiscent of the traditional arguments for the existence of God, particularly the ontological argument. It will be instructive to examine his general view of these arguments and his own analysis of the ontological argument.

Tillich argues that the traditional arguments, when considered as arguments, fail on two counts. "Both the concept of existence and the method of arguing to a conclusion are inadequate for the idea of God" (ST, 1:204). We have examined Tillich's reasons for dissociating the concept of existence from the nature of God. His second objection is rather obscure. Apparently, he thinks that when we start with certain facts about the world and conclude to the existence of God, we inevitably treat God as a *part* of the universe, as one being alongside others. And this, of course, contradicts his understanding of God as being-itself (ST, 1:205).

Tillich's positive analysis of the traditional arguments is:

> The arguments for the existence of God neither are arguments nor are they proof of the existence of God. They are expressions of the question of God which is implied in human finitude. This question is their truth; every answer they give is untrue. . . . The arguments for the existence of God analyze the human situation in such a way that the question of God appears possible and necessary (ST, 1:205–6).

This passage suggests that there is a *single* question which all of the traditional arguments considered by Tillich—ontological, cosmological, and teleological—express. This is misleading since Tillich regards the arguments as expressing what look like different questions. "The cosmological question of God is the question about that which ultimately makes courage possible, a courage which accepts and overcomes the anxiety of categorical finitude" (ST, 1:209). He later speaks of this question of the ground of courage as "the question of the ground of being" and contrasts it with the question expressed by the teleological argument. "The teleological argument formulates the question of the ground of meaning, just as the cosmological argument formulates the question of the ground of being" (ST, 1:210). Nowhere, to my knowledge, does Tillich say what question is formulated in the ontological argument aside from the general phrase "the question of God." I suggest that it would not be unfair to Tillich to characterize the ontological argument as formulating the question of the ground of thought. We now have what appear to be three questions: the ground of thought, the ground of being, and the ground of meaning. Undoubtedly, Tillich would view these as different approaches to a single reality, God. Hence, he can treat them as different versions of "the question of God." Aquinas does substantially the same thing when he treats each of his five arguments as an argument for the existence of God, even though the second proves a first cause, the third a necessary being, etc.

A second misleading feature of Tillich's positive analysis of the arguments is that it suggests that the arguments do not show the reality of God, since they only raise the question of God. Of course, for Tillich, the arguments do not prove the existence of a highest being. This may be part of what he means when he says "every answer they give is untrue." But what about God as being-itself? Does the ontological argument show that being-itself *is?* Tillich never explicitly raises this question, but it is not difficult to determine what his answer must be. What is difficult is to explicate the reasoning which lies behind Tillich's acceptance of a form of the ontological argument for God— when God is taken as being-itself. That Tillich does regard the argument as correctly implying the reality of God is strongly suggested in this statement:

> The Anselmian statement that God is a necessary thought and that therefore this idea must have objective as well as subjective reality is valid in so far as thinking, by its very nature, implies an unconditional element which transcends subjectivity and objectivity, that is, a point of identity which makes the idea of truth possible. However, the statement is not valid if this unconditional element is understood as a highest being called God. The existence of such a highest being is not implied in the idea of truth (ST, 1:207).

This argument is extraordinarily difficult to comprehend. What he is suggesting is that if we view God as being-itself then Anselm is right when he argues that if God has subjective reality (in the mind) he must have objective reality as well. The reason Anselm is right is that *thinking* by its very nature entails that being-itself *is*. Being-itself, for Tillich, is the unconditional element which transcends subjectivity and objectivity and which makes truth possible. Another way of putting the basic point is that being-itself is the presupposition of thought and truth. Tillich's most cryptic statement of this doctrine is: "God is the presupposition of the question of God."[11]

It is significant that whenever Tillich gives his own analysis of the ontological argument he notes with favor Augustine's claims concerning truth (TC, 13). There are three points in Augustine's discussion that Tillich appro-

---

[11] Paul Tillich, *Theology of Culture* (New York: Oxford University Press, 1959), p. 13. Hereafter references to this work will appear in the text abbreviated as TC.

priates in his analysis. The first point concerns a kind of Platonic framework in which 'x is ϕ' is true only if (a) there is ϕ-ness, and (b) x participates in ϕ-ness. Point b entails that it is through ϕ-ness that x has ϕ. Given this framework, suppose we raise the question whether there is any ϕ-ness. That there *is* is a condition or presupposition of anything being ϕ. Hence, if we know that x is ϕ, we can know that there is ϕ-ness. Substitute *truth* for ϕ. The argument now is that anything being true or having truth presupposes truth-itself.

R. First then let us see this, whether, as Truth and true are two words, you hold that by these words two things are signified, or one thing. A. Two things, I hold. For, as Chastity is one thing, and that which is chaste, another, and many things in this manner; so I believe that Truth is one thing, and that which, being declared, is true, is another. . . . it is not from that which is chaste that Chastity arises, but that which is chaste from Chastity. So also, if anything is true, it is assuredly from Truth that it is true.[12]

The second point to note is that Tillich, like Augustine, identifies *Truth* with *God*. "For where I found truth, there I found my God, who is the Truth itself, . . ."[13] Truth itself, so Augustine argues, cannot possibly perish. His argument here is as follows: Suppose Truth itself did perish. It would then be *true* that Truth itself has perished. But nothing can be true if Truth itself has perished. Hence, it is logically impossible that Truth itself should perish.[14] This being so, Truth is eternal and unchangeable; hence, Truth is God. Tillich sometimes identifies being-itself, good-itself, and truth-itself (TC, 15). At other times he speaks of truth-

---

[12] *Soliloquies* I. 27.

[13] *Confessions* Bk. X. Ch. XXIV.   [14] *Soliloquies* II. 2.

itself and good-itself as manifestations of being-itself (ST, 1:207).

The third point to note is that the Soul discovers Truth within itself. In the *Soliloques* Augustine argues that Truth is in the Soul. Tillich interprets Augustine in the mystical tradition as asserting that God is present in man's soul and, consequently, immediately knowable.

The Franciscan school of 13th century scholasticism represented by Alexander of Hales, Bonaventura, and Matthew of Aquasparta developed the Augustinian solution, . . . Their whole emphasis was on the immediacy of the knowledge of God. According to Bonaventura, "God is most truly present to the very soul and immediately knowable"; He is knowable to Himself without media as the one which is common to all. For He is the principle of knowledge, the first truth, in the light of which everything else is known, as Matthew says. As such He is the identity of subject and object (TC, 13).

This point is important since it throws some light on Tillich's persistent claim that God transcends the split between subject and object. To be an object in the subject-object structure entails an ontological separation from the subject. But God, since he is present in both subject and object, transcends the ontological split between the two; he is the point of identity which unites them.

I believe that these three points are assumed by Tillich in his analysis of the ontological argument. To think what is true presupposes Truth (being-itself). Hence, being-itself, for Tillich, is the presupposition of thought. Because he holds this, Tillich argues that the ontological argument validly infers the reality of God (being-itself), not because of some peculiar feature of the thought that God exists but because thinking by its very nature presupposes being-itself. Hence, Tillich wants to construe the argument as not really an argument at all but as an analysis of what is presupposed in human thought. Speaking of the argument he says:

It is neither an argument, nor does it deal with the existence of God, although it often has been expressed in this form. It is the rational description of the relation of our mind to Being as such. Our mind implies *principles per se nota* which have immediate evidence whenever they are noticed: the transcendentalia, *esse, verum, bonum*. They constitute the Absolute in which the difference between knowing and known is not actual. This absolute as the principle of Being has absolute certainty. It is a necessary thought because it is the presupposition of all thought (TC, 15).

I should prefer to say that there are *two* arguments: the ontological argument as set forth by Anselm and Descartes, and the Augustine-Tillich argument which bears some tenuous relation to the argument formulated by Anselm and Descartes.[15] Be this as it may, the interesting and important point about Tillich's discussion of the ontological argument is that it presupposes a kind of Platonic framework in which every being participates in being-itself. However, the crucial question is whether there is any such entity as being-itself. Tillich's positive analysis of the ontological argument does not disclose a new argument for being-itself. Rather, he asserts but does not give an argument for the claim that the ontological argument, when properly understood, shows that the reality of being-itself is presupposed by thought.

The main argument we have uncovered for the reality of God (being-itself) seems to rest on the impossibility that

---

[15] In Augustine it seems possible to distinguish the ontological argument from the argument from truth. See William Pearson Tolley, *The Idea of God in the Philosophy of St. Augustine* (New York: Richard R. Smith, Inc., 1930), pp. 82–87.

nothing (absolute nonbeing) should *be* or *exist.* 'Nothing exists' is contradictory since it attributes being even to nothing (absolute nonbeing). This being so, it is necessarily true either that some conditioned entity exists or that some unconditioned entity exists. But it is not necessary that any conditioned entity exists since we can imagine the negation of every thing (conditioned entity) that *is.* Hence, it is necessary that some unconditioned entity or element exists. But being-itself is the only unconditioned entity since every other entity participates in nonbeing. Hence, being-itself (God) necessarily exists.

The final point I wish to make in this chapter is a criticism of the argument just stated. Tillich asserts, "If one asks why there *is* not nothing, one attributes being even to nothing" (ST, 1:163). I think this assertion is mistaken. First, consider the question "Why *is* there not nothing?" Tillich understands this question as attributing being even to nothing. But is not this a misunderstanding of what we are doing when we ask a question of this sort? If one asks why there *is* no Santa Claus, one surely does *not* attribute being even to Santa Claus. If one asks why there *is* not a flying elephant, one does *not* attribute being even to a flying elephant. Similarly, if one asks why there *is* not nothing, one does not attribute being even to nothing. It may be that the question "Why *is* there not nothing?" is *inappropriate* in the sense that no answer is possible. But one who asks that question cannot be accused of attributing being even to nothing.

Another way of seeing that Tillich's claim is mistaken is to see that it implies that the assertion 'Nothing is' is contradictory. 'Nothing is'—where *nothing* is taken as absolute nonbeing—is contradictory according to Tillich since it asserts the existence of what does not exist (nothing); it attributes being even to nothing. But what we are doing in asserting that nothing exists is denying that existence applies at all. To deny that existence applies at all is not to apply it. On Tillich's view 'nothing exists' is still an attempt to apply existence—this time to what does not exist (nothing). One consequence of Tillich's view is that every statement which has the form 'nothing is ϕ' is contradictory. (1) 'Nothing exists' is contradictory because it consists in the attribution of *existence* to what is not (nothing). Suppose we say (2) 'nothing is red.' On Tillich's view 2 is to be understood as the attribution of *red* to what does not exist (nothing). Now, if 2 is to be true what does not exist (nothing) must exist for 'x is red' can be true only if 'x exists' is true. Hence, 2 on Tillich's analysis implies that which *is not* must exist. But if 2 implies a contradiction, 2 is itself contradictory. But surely 2 is false, not *necessarily* false. For the same reason (3) 'nothing is faster than the speed of light' turns out to be contradictory on Tillich's view. But 3, far from being a contradiction, is *true*. Hence, Tillich's analysis of 1 is mistaken, for 1 does not assert the existence of what does not exist (nothing).

We have seen that Tillich's analysis of 'nothing is' is mistaken. What could possibly lead him to hold such a view? I am inclined to think that Tillich assimilates sentences of the form 'nothing is ϕ' to sentences of the form 'Eisenhower is ϕ.' That is, he seems to regard 'nothing' as the name of something (what does not exist). While they may have a similar grammatical form, the sentences mentioned above, as most philosophers are aware, are not of the same logical type. Consider (1) 'nothing is bald' and (2) 'Eisenhower is bald.' The latter can be understood as the predication or attribution of *baldness* to something (Eisenhower). But point 1, although grammatically similar to 2, cannot be understood as the predication or attribution of baldness to some entity named or referred to by 'nothing.' Point 1 must be understood as claiming that baldness cannot be truly predicated of anything. But, unless I have misunderstood Tillich, his view implies that if one asks why there *is* no bald thing, one implicitly asserts the existence of a bald thing. My suggestion is that his mistaken view may be the result of not noting the logical difference between the expression 'nothing' and a name.

In this chapter I have sought (1) to explain precisely what Tillich means when he says "God does not exist," (2) to exhibit reasons within the classical conception of God why Tillich is led to hold that the concept of existence is incompatible with the nature of God, and (3) to show that Tillich, nevertheless, implies that God not only exists but necessarily exists. If my discussion of these points is essentially correct, it follows that there is a rather fundamental incoherence in Tillich's theology. For on the one hand he holds that the concept of existence and the concept of God are incompatible; whereas, on the other hand he makes statements about God and formulates arguments about God which imply or presuppose that there *is* a God, that God *exists*. Clearly, he cannot have it both ways. To remove this, at least apparent, incoherence from his theology it seems to me that Tillichians must pursue one of two alternatives:

1. Give up the claim that God does not exist. This, of course, will mean that the concept of existence is no longer held to be incompatible with the nature of God. This, as perhaps Tillich realizes, is not easy to do in view

of the doctrine that in God there is no distinction between essence and existence. Again, there are but two alternatives:

  a) Show that "God exists" is meaningful (perhaps by treating 'exists' analogically) even though in God there is no distinction between essence and existence.

  b) Allow that the distinction between essence and existence applies even to God.

2. Show that the various statements that are made about God in Tillich's theology can be true even if 'God exists' is false or meaningless. Clearly, this will involve more than the pious avowal that they are symbolic or analogical, not literal. What is needed is a careful account of how it is that these statements can be true when one of their apparently essential implications or presuppositions happens to be false or meaningless.

≈IV≈

Signs and Symbols

IN CHAPTER I we noted that by identifying God and being-itself Tillich believes he can account both for the aspect of ultimacy and for the aspect of concreteness in the idea of God. The ontological claim that being-itself is beyond all limitations is the basis on which Tillich hopes to accommodate the element of ultimacy in the idea of God. The claim that every being participates in being-itself makes possible, Tillich thinks, a theory of religious symbols which adequately accounts for the element of concreteness in the idea of God. In this chapter and those that follow I propose to examine Tillich's theory of signs, symbols, and myths.

In order to assess Tillich's theory of religious symbols it is necessary to examine his general theory of signs and symbols. This is so because (1) the notion of a religious symbol is explained in comparison with and in contrast to non-religious symbols (artistic, political, etc.) and (2) the notion of a symbol is explained in comparison with and in contrast to the concept of a sign. Thus to understand Tillich's concept of a religious symbol we must understand his distinctions between symbols generally and signs.

The simplest way of expressing Tillich's view of signs and symbols is as follows:

1. If x is a sign then x *points* beyond itself to something else.
2. If x is a symbol then x *points* beyond itself to something else.
3. If x is a sign then x does *not participate* in the reality of that to which it points.
4. If x is a symbol then x does *participate* in the reality of that to which it points.

Points 1 and 2 express what signs and symbols have in common. The third and fourth express what, for Tillich, is the basic difference between signs and symbols. Points 1 and 3 are equivalent to 5; 2 and 4 are equivalent to 6.

5. If x is a sign then x points beyond itself but does not participate in the reality of that to which it points.
6. If x is a symbol then x points beyond itself and participates in the reality of that to which it points.

The problem, then, of understanding Tillich's general theory of signs and symbols seems to reduce to the problem of understanding what is meant by 5 and 6. And this in turn seems to wait upon our understanding of what Tillich means when he says of something that it *points to* something else, and what he means when he says of something that it *participates in* the reality of that to which it points. But before we explore these central questions, certain preliminary points must be considered.

First, it must be noted that Tillich's use of 'symbol' and 'sign' deviates from certain quite ordinary uses of these expressions. For example, the mathematical *symbol* '+' is not a symbol in Tillich's use of 'symbol'. "The mathematician has usurped the term 'symbol' for mathematical 'sign,' . . . The only thing we can do is to distinguish different groups, signs which are called symbols, and genuine symbols. The mathematical signs are signs which are wrongly called symbols" (TC, 55). Tillich's claim that, for example, '+' is wrongly called a symbol is incorrect. There is no misuse of the term 'symbol' when certain mathematical expressions are called symbols. But perhaps we can understand Tillich to be saying that given his own concept of a symbol, it would be wrong to call the mathematical expression '+' a symbol. Granting statements 5 and 6, the mathematical expression '+', Tillich would claim, is a sign, not a symbol.

Second, we must bear in mind a distinction which cuts across both signs and symbols. Tillich speaks of certain words as signs and other words as symbols. Religious and poetic language is, Tillich claims, largely symbolic language. Words like 'God' and 'Christ' are symbols. However, most words are merely signs. "Words in a language are signs for a meaning which they express" (TC, 55). Thus it is clear that there are *linguistic entities* which are signs, and others which are symbols. The distinction we must bear in mind is between *linguistic* signs and symbols and *non-linguistic* signs and symbols. The flag and the crucifix are examples for Tillich of non-linguistic symbols. The road sign and the red traffic light are examples of non-linguistic signs. Not only is it important to note that the distinction between linguistic and non-linguistic cuts across both signs and symbols, but we must also recognize that 5 is intended as a claim about both linguistic and non-linguistic signs, and 6 is intended as a claim about both linguistic and non-linguistic symbols. It remains to be seen whether these two fundamental claims can be interpreted and justified.

Third, I wish to point out what sort of statements 5 and 6 may be taken to be. If we understand these to be *pro-*

posals by Tillich of how he intends to use the terms 'sign' and 'symbol' then, apart from the problem of explaining what is meant by 'pointing to something beyond itself' and 'participating', there is little that can be said in a critical way about 5 or 6. If it should turn out that some entity, say the flag, does not participate (whatever that means) in what it points to (whatever that means), we must simply conclude that Tillich was mistaken in calling the flag a symbol. But I think we misunderstand Tillich if we construe these statements as mere proposals by Tillich of how he intends to use 'sign' and 'symbol'. These statements are attempts at stating the *essential nature* of a sign and a symbol, not remarks about word usage.

Perhaps the traditional notions of extension and intension will serve to clarify the status of 5 and 6. Where 'A' is a general term we may characterize the *extension* of 'A' as the set of all things which are A's. Thus, for example, the extension of 'German Shepherd dog' will be the set whose members are Rin-Tin-Tin, Strongheart, etc. We may understand the intension of 'A' as the set of properties a thing must have to be in the extension of 'A'.

It is important to note that we may be quite sure that certain entities fall within the extension of a term and that others fall outside of its extension even though we are quite unsure about the intension of that term. Thus we may be certain that Rin-Tin-Tin is, and Lassie is not, a member of the extension of 'German Shepherd dog' even though we are uncertain and unclear about the intension of 'German Shepherd dog'. Accordingly, my suggestion is that 5 and 6 are to be understood as attempts by Tillich to state the *intensions* of 'sign' and 'symbol', respectively. Moreover, as is the case with 'German Shepherd dog', Tillich is fairly clear about at least some members of the extensions of these two terms. And this fact provides us with a way of evaluating 5 and 6. For, if it should turn out that *the flag* or *the Christ* does not exhibit the properties mentioned in 6, then it will follow that 6 is *incorrect*. Thus our task with regard to 5 and 6 is twofold: we must endeavor to explain and interpret these statements, and we must determine whether they are justified by the examples Tillich gives of signs and symbols.

Finally, it should be noted that Tillich ascribes several features to symbols, and sometimes uses one or more of these features to distinguish symbols from signs. Thus in addition to the basic claim that symbols participate in the reality of that to which they point, Tillich claims that symbols (1) open up levels of reality which are otherwise closed to us, (2) unlock dimensions and elements of our soul which correspond to the dimensions and elements of reality, (3) cannot be produced or replaced intentionally and (4) grow and die. I strongly suspect that Tillich would ascribe *none* of these features to signs. He explicitly mentions signs in connection with 3 and 4 and remarks that signs are established by human convention and thus may be produced or replaced intentionally.

Every symbol has a special function which is just *it* and cannot be replaced by more or less adequate symbols. This is different from signs, for signs can always be replaced. If one finds that a green light is not so expedient as perhaps a blue light (this is not true, but could be true), then we put on a blue light, and nothing is changed. . . . As different from signs, symbols are born and die. Signs are consciously invented and removed. This is a fundamental difference (TC, 58).

As we shall see, some of the features of these points are perhaps more helpful in explicating the distinction between signs and symbols than is the concept of participation.

As I indicated, Tillich asserts that the one decisive respect in which symbols are similar to signs is that both signs and symbols point beyond themselves to something else. Our first problem then, is to explain what Tillich means by the phrase "points beyond itself to something else." But why is it necessary to explicate this phrase? Is it not simple and clear enough as it stands? There is no question but that the expression 'pointing to' is a quite ordinary expression with a fairly clear meaning, in fact with a number of fairly clear meanings. And clearly, the sense of the expression 'points to,' which undoubtedly leads Tillich to use it in his statement about signs and symbols, is its quite ordinary sense of 'directing our attention to', 'indicating'. Thus the road sign with a curved arrow directs our attention to, indicates a curve in the road. A curve in the road is the 'something else' to which a road sign points. But it would be premature to conclude that all the entities which Tillich classifies as signs or symbols exhibit just *this sense* of 'pointing to' in relation to the objects of which they are signs or symbols. Hence, it is important to consider the various kinds of signs and symbols and to raise the question of what Tillich means when he speaks of them as "pointing to something else." For my purpose it will suffice to examine certain cases of *linguistic* signs and symbols. As we shall see, it is not a simple matter to specify what Tillich means when he says, for example, that a word (linguistic sign) *points to* its meaning. In fact, I shall suggest two possible interpretations of what Tillich might mean by the claim that a word points to its meaning. According to the first interpretation—which I shall call "view A"—"pointing to" is to be understood as *referring*, and the meaning of a word, in a given context of utterance, is to be identified with that to which the word refers in that context. According to the second view—which I shall call "view B"—"pointing to" is to be understood as *signifying*, and the meaning of a word is *not* to be identified with its referent. Moreover, although at least one of Tillich's remarks suggests that he holds view A, I shall argue (1) that the theory of meaning presupposed by view A is untenable and (2) that, if we are interested in developing Tillich's remarks into a coherent theory of signs and symbols, view B is the most promising interpretation to make of his claims.

Concerning linguistic signs, we may begin by noting that Tillich regards both words, presumably written or uttered, and the written letters of the alphabet as signs. His view is that the written letters, 'A', 'B', etc., are signs and their *sounds* are that to which they point. Will "direct our attention to" do here? Written words, however, do not point to their sounds but to their *meanings*. Thus of letters and words Tillich says, "They point beyond themselves to sounds and meanings" (DF, 41). In one of the *rare*, I am sorry to say, passages in which he discusses a particular example of a linguistic sign Tillich remarks: "Words in a language are signs for a meaning which they express. The word 'desk' is a sign which points to something quite different—namely, the thing on which a paper is lying and at which we might be looking" (TC, 55). What are we to make of this remark? In developing view A, I propose the following interpretation. Tillich appears to be claiming that the meaning of the word 'desk', on the particular occasion he is using that word, is a particular desk ("the thing on which a paper is lying . . ."). If this is correct, 'pointing to' is to be understood as *referring*. For the sense in which the word 'desk', as he uses it, "points to" a particular desk is simply that the word, in that context, *refers* (more accurately, is being *used to refer*) to that particular desk. According to this view, then, we are (1) to understand "pointing to" as *referring* and (2) to identify the meaning of an expression—in a given context—with that to which the expression refers—in that context. Thus, in the appropriate context of utterance, the expression 'dog' in 'My dog is a German Shepherd' will point to—denote, refer to—a particular member of the extension of 'dog'; namely, my own dog, Heidi. And, furthermore, in this context of utterance *the meaning* of 'dog' is my dog, Heidi.

If view A is a correct interpretation of Tillich's claim that a word points to its meaning, then whatever else we may wish to say about Tillich's theory of signs and symbols, I think we must say that it rests on a theory of meaning which is untenable. There are quite strong objections to such a theory. I shall mention three.

First, it would seem to follow from view A that in the appropriate context the meaning of 'dog' and the meaning of 'Heidi' will be one and the same, for each expression will refer or point to one and the same animal. Now it is paradoxical enough to think of a proper name as having a meaning, but it is doubly paradoxical to be told that a general term may, in a given context, have the *same meaning* as a proper name. In general, if 'a' has the same meaning as 'b' then from 'a is ϕ' we can validly infer 'b is ϕ'. But clearly from the statement 'Heidi is a German Shepherd' we cannot validly infer the statement 'That dog is a German Shepherd'. Hence, even though 'dog'—'that dog'—and 'Heidi' may be used to refer to (point to) one and the same animal, it is a mistake to think that they have the *same meaning*.

Second, it would seem to follow that the meaning of a general term would vary from one utterance to another. Consider a context in which the following true statements are made: (*a*) 'The bachelor by the wall is Smith' and (*b*) 'The bachelor by the door is Jones'. In Tillich's theory—assuming that he holds view A—the meaning of 'bachelor' changes from *a* to *b*, for in *a* 'bachelor' (really, 'the bachelor') refers to (points to) Smith and in *b* it refers to Jones. But clearly a word may alter its referent without altering its meaning. The word 'bachelor' means the same in *a* and *b* even though it is being used in *a* to refer to Smith, and in *b* to refer to Jones.

Third, it must be noted that not all words in our language can properly be said to refer or point to something else. Proper names and general terms can be used to point to or refer to something else. But what do the words 'if', 'and', or 'maybe' point to? These words are not used to denote or refer to any entities. But, of course, they are not meaningless. Thus any theory that identifies the meaning of a word with that to which the word (linguistic sign) points (refers) is unsatisfactory.

The point to which each of these objections is directed is the *identification* of the meaning of an expression with that to which, in a certain context of utterance, the expression refers. Once this point is denied the three objections no longer apply. For if the meaning of 'dog' in "My dog is a German Shepherd" is distinguished from that to which 'dog' refers, in that context of utterance, then (*a*) the meaning of 'dog' in that context need not be identical with the meaning or referent of "Heidi" and (*b*) the meaning of 'dog' can remain constant even though its referent changes from one context of utterance to another. Also, (*c*) words such as 'if', 'and', and 'maybe' are not rendered meaningless by the fact that they do not refer to something beyond themselves.

I have discussed this rather primitive version of the reference theory of meaning—namely, the version which *identifies* the meaning of a word with that to which, in a given context of utterance, the word points or refers—because it is entailed by view A, and view A is suggested by Tillich's remark about the word 'desk'. On this interpretation of Tillich what a word 'points to' is what, in a given context, that word *refers to*. The difficulty is that Tillich seems to identify the meaning of a word with that to which the word points. Given this identification *and* the interpretation of "points to" as *refers to* we are then committed to an untenable version of the reference theory of meaning. If we are interested in developing an interpretation of Tillich that avoids this unhappy end, then I suggest that we abandon the view that what a linguistic expression points to in a given context is that to which the expression refers in that context. Thus I suggest that view A be discarded.

Of course, having abandoned *referring* as an interpretation of "pointing to", we must now find another interpretation for Tillich's claim that signs and symbols point beyond themselves to something else. Concerning words—one class of linguistic signs—we know that the *meaning* of a word is, on Tillich's view, that to which the word points. Accordingly, I propose first, that we regard the *primary sense* or *literal meaning* of a given word as what Tillich intends to designate as that to which the word *points*. Thus, for example, the literal meaning of 'bachelor', namely, *an un-*

married adult male, is, on this interpretation of Tillich, that to which the word 'bachelor' points. Secondly, I suggest that we interpret Tillich's notion of 'pointing to' as *signifying.* Hence, we shall say that 'bachelor' signifies (points to) *an unmarried adult male.* On view B, the word 'bachelor' will have the same meaning, signification, even though in different utterances it is being used to refer to different men. Finally, I propose that we employ "signifies" as a substitute for Tillich's notion of "points to" wherever the latter occurs. Thus both non-linguistic and linguistic entities—whether signs or symbols—may point to (i.e., signify) something else.

Before considering the distinction Tillich endeavors to draw between symbols and signs, it will be instructive to investigate more fully his concept of a sign. The following examples will aid our investigation.

1. A road sign with a curved arrow signifies a curve in the road.
2. A red traffic light signifies the order to stop.
3. Nimbus clouds signify rain.
4. Smoke signifies fire.
5. The word 'bachelor' signifies an unmarried adult male.
6. The word 'shepherd' signifies a man employed in tending, feeding, and guarding sheep.
7. The American flag signifies the American nation.
8. The sacramental bread and wine signify the body and blood of Christ.

(Having adopted view B as the most promising interpretation of Tillich, I have used 'signifies' rather than 'points to' in each of these examples. There is little doubt that Tillich would regard each example as a case of an entity pointing beyond itself to something else.)

As we noted earlier, if x is a sign or a symbol then, according to Tillich's theory, x points to (signifies) something else. But does Tillich hold the converse—that is, does he hold that if x points to (signifies) something else then x is a sign or a symbol? To my knowledge, Tillich never explicitly states the converse, never explicitly states that if x points to y then x is a sign or a symbol. Of course, failing to assert the converse is not equivalent to denying the converse. But I think that given his remarks about the fundamental nature of signs and symbols Tillich is committed to the denial of the converse. That is, he is committed to the view that something may point to something else and yet be neither a sign nor a symbol. Indeed, both nimbus clouds and smoke, as mentioned in examples 3 and 4, do not, I believe, qualify as signs or symbols on Tillich's theory.

There is, it seems to me, a rather important distinction between two classes of signs, a distinction which is not accounted for in Tillich's theory. Signs, Tillich insists, are always *conventional*. "A red light and the stopping of cars have essentially no relation to each other, but conventionally they are united as long as the convention lasts" (DF, 41). ". . . signs can be replaced for reasons of expediency or convention, while symbols cannot" (DF, 42). "Signs are consciously invented and removed" (TC, 58). These and other remarks make it clear that Tillich's view is that if x is a *sign* of y then the relation of signification in which x stands to y is *conventional*.

However, I think there are *natural,* as well as conventional, signs. Nimbus clouds are a sign of rain. Smoke is a sign of fire. But the relation between nimbus clouds and rain, as between smoke and fire, was not devised *or* decreed by man, it was discovered by him. We decree that four bells will signify fire, but we do not decree that smoke will signify fire. That smoke is a sign of fire is something we have discovered. A red light and the stopping of cars, as Tillich remarks, have essentially no relation to each other. But nimbus clouds and rain do have a natural relation to each other. Hence, it appears that what I have called 'natural signs' are not really signs at all in Tillich's theory. If this is correct, then unless nimbus clouds and smoke are symbols for Tillich, it follows that on his theory not all entities which point to (signify) something else are either signs or symbols.

It is fairly clear, I think, that Tillich would not regard nimbus clouds, and other natural 'signs', as symbols since they lack some of the essential characteristics Tillich ascribes to symbols. For example, as we noted, he says that a symbol "opens up levels of reality which otherwise are closed for us" (DF, 42). We would be hard put to imagine a level of reality revealed to us by nimbus clouds which we could not get at in any other way. It may make some sense to think of a great painting as doing this, but hardly a nimbus cloud. Thus we may conclude that although signification (pointing to) is a necessary condition for x being a sign or symbol, it is not a sufficient condition. 'Natural signs' signify what they are signs of, but they fail to satisfy Tillich's requirement for a sign or a symbol.

What the above discussion has shown is that Tillich's concept of a sign is such that for x to be a sign, x must not only signify something else (y) but the relation of signification that x has to y must be *conventional,* the result of human invention. Furthermore, we have seen that it is the *conventional* nature of the relation between the sign and what it is a sign of that leads Tillich to remark that signs may be "changed arbitrarily according to the demands of expediency" (ST, 1:239). Collecting these features together we may unpack Tillich's concept of a sign as follows:

X is a sign of *y* just in case:

a) *x* signifies *y*,

b) the relation of signification that *x* has to *y* is conventional, and

c) *x* may be replaced by something else as a sign of *y* for reasons of mere expediency.

Of our list of examples, 1, 2, 5, and 6 involve signs on Tillich's theory. The last two involve symbols. And, as we have seen, 3 and 4 are cases in which neither signs nor symbols are involved.

Although more needs to be said about Tillich's notion of a sign, we can do this best in the course of exploring Tillich's distinctions between signs and symbols. However, one point must be noted here concerning the third feature in Tillich's concept of a sign noted above; namely, the replacement of a sign by something else for reasons of mere expediency. Tillich remarks: ". . . signs can always be replaced. If one finds that a green light is not so expedient as perhaps a blue light (this is not true, but could be true), then we simply put on a blue light, and nothing is changed" (TC, 58). It would be a mistake to think that the replaceable character of the sign implies that its choice is arbitrary, that something else would have done just as well. For clearly in the case of non-linguistic signs, *x* may have natural properties which render it more suitable to signify *y* than anything else. It may be that three or five bells would have done just as well as a sign of fire as four. But the curved arrow of the road sign renders it more suitable as a sign of a curve in the road than some other configuration. The kicking motion performed by the referee on the football field as a sign of a roughing the kicker penalty is a more suitable motion than any other for what it signifies. (Compare also the appropriateness of the signal for a clipping penalty.) The red light may have natural properties which render it more suitable as a sign of the order to stop than a light of another color. Furthermore, some linguistic signs may have properties rendering them more suitable as signs of what they signify than other linguistic expressions. Consider onomatopoetic words, such as 'buzz' or 'bobwhite', and compound words, such as 'foxhound', 'sheepdog' and the like. Hence, the conventional character of the relation of signification in which the sign x stands to y is not to be understood as implying that the choice of x, rather than z, to signify y was arbitrary, without good reason.

The replaceable character of the sign for reasons of expediency must be understood as follows. Suppose color blindness with respect to red and green were to become much more prominent than it now is. It would then, I suppose, be expedient to replace either the red or green color of the traffic light—by some other color. Tillich is suggesting that if x is a sign of y, and such reasons of expediency develop, we may replace x by z with the result that z now is taken to signify y, and nothing is changed. As we shall see, when x is a symbol of y, not merely a sign, Tillich's view is that the replacement of x by some other symbol z can be accomplished only if something *significant is changed*.

As I have indicated, Tillich claims that the fundamental difference between signs and symbols is that symbols, unlike signs, participate in the reality of that to which they point (DF, 42). He sometimes expresses this by saying that symbols, unlike signs, participate in the meaning and power of the reality to which they point. It is apparent that our major problem here is to understand what it means or could mean to say of anything that it *participates* in the meaning, power, or reality of that to which it points. What is this relationship of participation, setting symbols apart from signs which signify but do not participate in that which they signify?

One possibility is that Tillich is drawing attention to a *similarity* between a symbol and what it signifies which does not hold between a sign and that which it signifies. But what sort of *similarity* might this be? First, let us consider the possibility that the symbol bears a structural similarity to what it symbolizes. Could this be what Tillich means by participation? However, it is clear that this will not work since the road sign with its curved arrow—which is a sign, not a symbol—bears a structural similarity to a curve in the road; whereas, the flag—which is a symbol for Tillich, not a sign—apparently bears little or no structural similarity to the nation which it symbolizes. Hence, similarity in terms of structure is not a likely candidate for what Tillich means by saying that the symbol participates in that to which it points.

A second and more fruitful possibility is that the similarity in question is to be discovered in the way human beings treat the symbol. That is, we respond to, feel toward, and treat the symbol in ways essentially similar to the ways we respond to, feel toward, and treat that for which the symbol stands. Consider the example of the flag, which, according to Tillich, we accept as a symbol of our nation. The suggestion is that the flag participates in the nation in the sense that it shares in the dignity we attribute to the nation. Consider our reaction if we came upon a man washing his car, using the American flag as a washrag. This act would be considered an attack on the dignity of our nation. "The man has absolutely no respect for his country!" might be the appropriate thing to say. Thus there seems to be a similarity between the flag and the nation in the sense that many of the appropriate ways of responding to the nation are the appropriate ways of responding to the flag. It is also clear that religious symbols have this character—ordinary elements such as bread or wine when viewed as symbols of Christ's body are treated with the sort of reverence and awe one might feel toward that which the symbol signifies. Perhaps, then, this is the sort of thing that Tillich has in mind when he says that symbols *participate* in the reality that is symbolized. That is, x participates in y means that x is similar to y in the sense that human beings feel toward and treat x in the same way they do y. Of course, simply by virtue of the fact that x and y are *different* sorts of things there always will be modes of treatment appropriate to the one but not to the other. Thus we *fold* the flag, we do not fold the nation. We *raise* the flag, we do not, at least in the same sense, raise the nation. But all that is required is that in certain important ways we feel toward and treat x in the same way as y.

Concerning the above suggestion, I wish to make three remarks: (1) As a characterization of the various examples of symbols Tillich provides, it seems essentially correct—a symbol is similar to the reality symbolized in terms of the ways in which human beings respond to each. (2) This fact about symbols is not a basis for an adequate distinction between signs and symbols—at the very least it raises questions for which no clear answers can be found in Tillich's writings. (3) This fact about symbols does not seem to be regarded by Tillich as an *explication* of the participation of symbols in what they symbolize but as a *consequence* of that participation. I shall now elaborate each of these remarks in some detail.

I have already indicated how this similarity of emotional response holds between the flag and the nation and between religious symbols and the divine. That it holds of all symbols is not, I think, an empirical question for Tillich. That is, on Tillich's theory, it is a necessary, although not a sufficient, condition of something being a symbol for us that we respond to it in ways basically similar to the ways we respond to what is symbolized. Although it may be impossible to prove this for symbols generally, it can, I believe, be demonstrated for what is for Tillich the most important class of symbols, namely *religious symbols.* The proof follows from our conclusions concerning ultimate concern in Chapter I. There we saw that Tillich regards religious symbols or sacred objects as those concrete entities which become the foci of ultimate concern. But, as we also saw, ultimate concern is basically directed at the ultimate, being-itself, and, as we shall see, that to which religious symbols point either directly or indirectly, on Tillich's theory, is the ultimate, being-itself. Hence, it follows that the appropriate way of responding (i.e., with ultimate concern) to that to which religious symbols point— the ultimate—is, in fact, the appropriate way of responding to religious symbols. It is quite likely that Tillich's view of non-religious symbols would be patterned after his explicit view about religious symbols. Thus I think we may safely regard it as a feature of Tillich's theory of symbols that certain important ways of feeling toward and treating the symbol are similar to or identical with certain important ways of feeling toward and treating that which the symbol symbolizes or stands for.

The reason why this identity of response to symbol and what is symbolized does not seem to be an adequate basis for differentiating symbols from signs is that it also seems to characterize certain signs. To a man in a building the sound of four bells may evoke fear, readiness for flight, etc., which would be evoked by the presence of what is signified by the four bells, namely, fire. Of course, we could say, and perhaps Tillich would allow this, that what is a sign in certain contexts may be a symbol in others—thus when we hear the four bells in the course of a firedrill the four bells perhaps function only as a sign; whereas, when we hear them under other conditions they may function as a symbol. But there seems to be a serious objection to this move. Symbols, Tillich tells us, open up levels of reality, as well as dimensions of the soul, which cannot be approached in any other way. But it is very odd indeed to think of a certain occurrence of four bells doing this. Moreover, symbols grow and die, but a certain occurrence of four bells does not grow and die—at least not in any way different from the occurrence of any other sound. Hence, I conclude that the identity of responses to x and to what x points to (signifies) does not provide an adequate basis for differentiating symbols from signs. If I am right about this, then it follows that if we interpret 'x participates in y' to mean 'x is similar to y in the sense that human beings feel toward and treat x in the same way they do y', the notion of *participation* is unable to do the task Tillich assigns to it; namely, providing an adequate basis for distinguishing symbols from signs.

Finally, it must be noted that Tillich himself seems to view the similarity of emotional response as a *consequence* of the participation of x in y rather than as an *explication* of that participation. Thus he writes:

> . . . the flag participates in the power of the king or the nation for which it stands and which it symbolizes. There has, therefore, been a fight . . . as to how to behave in the presence of the flag. This would be meaningless if the flag did not participate as a symbol in the power of that which it symbolizes (TC, 55).

If the way we behave toward the symbol is a consequence of the symbol's participation in what it symbolizes, it is a mistake to explicate the latter in terms of the former. Hence, it would seem incorrect to take 'participation' to *mean* a similarity between symbol and what is symbolized in terms of the ways in which human beings respond to them.

In Chapter I, I had occasion to distinguish between (1) Tillich's phenomenological description of religious experience and (2) the elaborate ontology that he employs in explaining the phenomena of religious experience. This distinction is relevant to our attempt to explicate 'participation' in terms of similarity of emotional response. The basic reason this attempt fails is that similarity of emotional response belongs to the level of the phenomenological description of religious experience; whereas *participation* is, for Tillich, an ontological category and therefore belongs to the level of ontological explanation. That human beings respond to symbols in ways fundamentally similar to the ways in which they respond to what the symbols signify is one of the phenomena of religion which Tillich wishes to interpret and explain. Tillich's explanation for this phenomenon, simply put, is that symbols participate in that to which they point. Clearly, it will not do now to explicate 'participate' in such a fashion that the purportedly explanatory statement, "Symbols participate in that to which they point," is reduced to the descriptive statements it was intended to interpret and explain. It would seem, then, that we must explore Tillich's use of 'participation' as an *ontological concept,* if we are to explicate what is meant by his claim that the symbol participates in the reality of that to which it points.

Tillich introduces the concept of participation as an ontological element—a property or quality which is exhibited by every being. Thus if there exists any being which fails to exhibit a certain property, that property cannot be an ontological element. Within Tillich's metaphysical system there are six ontological elements divided into three pairs: individualization and participation, dynamics and form, and freedom and destiny. One wonders, however, how all of these can be ontological elements. It may make sense to say that every human being exhibits freedom. But can we seriously maintain that a stone or a grain of sand has freedom? Tillich is aware of this difficulty. He recognizes that all of the six concepts apply, in their primary meaning, only to man. However, they may be called ontological elements because *analogies* to these concepts apply to non-human things. Thus what Tillich attempts to do is to define or characterize each element (e.g., participation, or freedom) in such a way that it applies literally only to man. Then he claims that a non-human thing is such that even though it does not exhibit what 'participation', for example, designates in man, what it does exhibit sufficiently resembles participation in man so as to justify the extension of the concept of participation to everything that is. This implies, of course, that as an ontological element, 'participation' has no *single* sense or meaning in which Tillich is prepared to ascribe it to every being.

117

Perhaps the fundamental difficulty inherent in Tillich's discussion of *participation* is his failure to explain the many different uses which this term has in his system. Participation as a structure in man's life apparently includes the various relationships a human being has with other human beings and with his world. But Tillich recognizes that the concept has many functions or uses in his system. "A symbol participates in the reality it symbolizes; the knower participates in the known; the lover participates in the beloved; the existent participates in the essences which make it what it is, under the conditions of existence;" etc. (ST, 1: 177). Finally, Tillich says, "Every relation includes a kind of participation. This is true even of indifference or hostility. Nothing can make one hostile in which one does not somehow participate, perhaps in the form of being excluded from it. And nothing can produce the attitude of indifference whose existence has not made some difference" (ST, 1:177). It would seem that when Tillich says 'x participates in y' all we can infer from this is that x is related in some way or other (perhaps simply by being excluded from y) to y. What he needs to do is specify the relation he has in mind, since 'participation' is a kind of general duty word good for any relation whatever. But Tillich fails to specify the relation at crucial points. And I am afraid that his failure to specify the relation extends to the very point which we are seeking to interpret and understand; namely, the sense in which symbols do, and signs do not, *participate* in that to which they point. His fundamental claim about what distinguishes symbols from signs is *informative* only if Tillich tells us what relation it is that symbols have to the reality to which they point, but signs do not have to the reality to which they point. It is our misfortune that Tillich, to my knowledge, never does this. Hence, his fundamental distinction between signs and symbols is uninformative. All it tells us is that there is *some relation* that symbols have to what they signify and signs do not have to what they signify. The interesting and crucial question for our inquiry, What is that relation? Tillich nowhere answers. In fact, it follows from his discussion of 'participation', quoted above, that there is a sense in which *both* symbols and signs participate in that for which they stand; for they both exhibit the *same* relation of *pointing to* that of which they are symbols or signs. For he explicitly claims that every relation includes a kind of participation. Apparently, then, we are to understand that both symbols and signs 'participate' in something else by virtue of the fact that they point to it. However, symbols also participate in some other sense as well. But this further sense is left unclarified. Until some clarification is given it seems to me that Tillich's fundamental distinction between signs and symbols is quite uninformative.

In view of the failure of the notion of participation to do the job that Tillich assigns to it—namely, provide a basic distinction between signs and symbols—we had best turn to some of the other features that Tillich ascribes to symbols in the hope of using one or more of them as a basis for distinguishing symbols from signs. There are, as we noted earlier, four such features. Symbols, Tillich says,

1. open up levels of reality which are otherwise closed to us
2. unlock dimensions and elements of our soul which correspond to the dimensions and elements of reality
3. cannot be produced or replaced intentionally
4. grow and die

Of these four, the most promising for our purpose, it seems to me, are 3 and 4. Perhaps an examination of these two features will enable us to understand why Tillich classes certain entities as signs and others as symbols.

The first point to note is that 4 purports to be a *positive* characterization of symbols, whereas 3 is *negative*, telling us that symbols cannot be consciously or intentionally produced or replaced. The purpose of 3 is to set symbols apart from signs which, for Tillich, are intentionally produced and may be intentionally removed or replaced. Since symbols then, are neither produced nor replaced in the way in which signs are, the question arises as to how something becomes a symbol or ceases to be one. The purpose of 4 is to provide a positive answer to this question. Symbols, unlike signs, are not consciously produced or replaced, instead they grow and die. That this is how we are to understand 3 and 4 is clear from the following remark:

No symbol can be replaced when used in its special function. So one asks rightly, "How do symbols arise, and how do they come to an end?" As different from signs, symbols are born and die. Signs are consciously invented and removed. This is a fundamental difference (TC, 58).

Earlier, we noted that Tillich's concept of a sign seems to be such that *x* is a sign of *y* just in case

a) *x* signifies *y*

b) the relation of signification that *x* has to *y* is conventional

c) *x* may be replaced as a sign of *y* for reasons of mere expediency

Perhaps we can clarify Tillich's concept of a symbol by using 3 and 4 in connection with our suggested analysis, however partial it may be, of Tillich's notion of a sign.

First, we must say that every symbol exhibits the first feature of a sign—namely, signifying. Hence, if x is a symbol of y then x signifies y. But what about b? Is the relation of signification that x (the symbol) has to y *conventional?* Some of Tillich's remarks suggest a negative answer. But this is a difficult matter. Surely Hitler, or his underlings, *chose* the swastika as a symbol of his movement. Prior to his decision the swastika—which existed as early as the civilization of Troy—did not *signify* the Nazi Party. The same may be said of a national flag. It was a recent act of the Canadian Parliament which established the red maple leaf emblem on a white background as the flag of Canada— thus establishing the relationship of signification between the new flag and the Canadian nation. Hence, it cannot be denied that some entities which are symbols for Tillich signify what they do signify as a result of human convention. We may, therefore, subject to certain qualifications to be noted later, ascribe to at least some symbols the second feature in our analysis of Tillich's concept of a sign.

The third feature in our analysis of Tillich's concept of a sign is explicitly rejected by Tillich as a description of symbols. But here again, we must move carefully. It is not that symbols cannot be removed, they sometimes are. The old Canadian flag has been removed as a symbol of the Canadian nation, and a new one has taken its place. Rather, it is that a symbol cannot be removed for reasons of mere expediency. When a symbol is removed it is because of a significant change either in what is symbolized or in the relation of the group to what is symbolized. Thus, of the flag as a symbol, Tillich remarks: ". . . it cannot be replaced except after an historic catastrophe that changes the reality of the nation which it symbolizes" (DF, 42).

No such catastrophe seems to have occurred to the Canadian nation. But perhaps the gradual, but nevertheless, significant change in the Canadian nation vis-à-vis England would suffice for Tillich. Hence, we may say that in contrast to the sign, a symbol, for Tillich, can be replaced or removed only if there has been a significant change in what is signified by the symbol or in the group's relation to what is signified.

Tillich claims that symbols, unlike signs, cannot be intentionally invented or removed. Perhaps now we are in a position to elucidate that remark. I have argued that, where x is a symbol and y is what x symbolizes, the relation of signification that x bears to y can be conventional, intentionally established. But, of course, if that were the whole story x would be a sign rather than a symbol. For x to be a symbol of y there must be an *unconscious* acceptance of and response to the proposed signification of y by x. In fact, the *conscious decision* to establish a relation of signification between x and y may itself be the result of some deep unconscious need for such a symbol. Thus of symbols Tillich says:

They grow out of the individual or collective unconscious and cannot function without being accepted by the unconscious dimension of our being. Symbols which have an especially social function, as poetical and religious symbols, are created or at least accepted by the collective unconscious of the group in which they appear (DF, 43).

Again, he remarks:

"Out of what womb are symbols born?" Out of the womb which is usually called today the "group unconscious" or "collective unconscious," or whatever you want to call it—out of a group which acknowledges, in this thing, this word, this flag, or whatever it may be, its own being. It is not invented intentionally; and even if somebody would try to invent a symbol, as sometimes happens, then it becomes a symbol only if the unconscious of a group says "yes" to it. It means that something is opened up by it in the sense which I have just described. Now this implies further that in the moment in which this inner situation of the human group to a symbol has ceased to exist, then the symbol dies. The symbol does not "say" anything any more. In this way, all of the polytheistic gods have died; the situation in which they were born, has changed or does not exist any more, and so the symbols died. But these are events which cannot be described in terms of intention and invention (TC, 58).

It would seem, then, that a symbol, for Tillich, must fulfill some unconscious need in the group. Moreover, when, for whatever reasons, the unconscious need of the group changes, the symbol may die.

The connection Tillich draws between symbols and the "unconscious dimension of our being" is reminiscent of Freud's theory of symbols. In Freud's theory a particular object, for example, a doll, may become a symbol of some significant figure in a child's environment, perhaps the mother. The doll then becomes the focus of actions and feelings, which express unconscious wishes that are symbolically directed at the mother. Clearly, the doll as a symbol has, in this case, certain profound connections with the child's unconscious life, connections that ordinary signs lack. Moreover, the replacement or removal of the doll as a symbol can occur only when the inner situation undergoes some significant change.

If I am right in suggesting that Tillich's concept of a symbol is in certain ways like Freud's, it appears necessary to qualify my earlier suggestion that the relation of signification between the symbol, x, and what is symbolized, y, may be *conventional*. For while the fact that the doll signifies the mother for the child is not a case of signification due to non-human nature—as, for example, is the case between smoke and fire—it is misleading to speak of it as *conventional,* if by 'conventional' we mean 'resulting from *conscious* human decision'. For the child may, on the conscious level, be completely unaware that the doll signifies —for her—her mother. In the light of this possibility, we may regard the relation of signification between symbol and what is symbolized as due either to conscious human decision *or* to unconscious needs, and sometimes both.

As a partial analysis of Tillich's concept of a symbol I suggest the following: x is a symbol of y just in case

 a) x signifies y

 b) the relation of signification that x has to y is conventional and/or due to unconscious needs

 c) x can be replaced or removed only if y or the group's relation to y has undergone some significant change

 d) x is accepted and responded to on the unconscious level

This analysis is partial in at least two respects. First, it does not take into account what Tillich asserts to be the basic feature of the symbol; namely, its *participation* in that which it signifies. The reason for this is simply that I have not been able to explicate Tillich's notion of participation in any way so as to render it useful in the understanding of his concept of a symbol. Furthermore, as I have sought to show, in Tillich's system the term 'participation' is a general duty word good for any relation whatever. Hence, his use of the term as a fundamental feature of symbols, distinguishing them from signs, is informative only if Tillich tells us what particular relation he means to ascribe to symbols but not to signs. But Tillich does not do this.

Hence, it seems pointless to use *participation* in the course of elucidating Tillich's concept of a symbol.

Second, the analysis does not take into account either of the following features Tillich ascribes to symbols: symbols open up levels of reality which are otherwise closed to us; symbols unlock dimensions and elements of our soul which correspond to the dimensions and elements of reality. The reason I have not included these features is because neither seems to be a *general* feature of symbols, that is, of the examples Tillich provides of symbols. What level of reality, for example, does the flag open up? What dimension of the soul does it unlock? The notions of "levels of reality" and "dimensions of the soul" are far too unclear in themselves to be helpful in clarifying Tillich's idea of a symbol. Tillich says that the levels of reality opened up by a symbol "otherwise are closed to us." Perhaps this is an apt way of speaking about a few great works of art, but it will hardly do for the national flag. At best these two features will apply only to some of Tillich's examples of symbols. Hence, I have made no effort to include them in my analysis of Tillich's concept of a symbol.

The analysis I have given does suggest that being accepted and responded to by the "unconscious level of our being" is a *sine qua non* for something being a symbol. If this is correct then it follows that x may be a symbol of y for one group, but only a sign for another group. It may evoke an unconscious acceptance and response in the first group, but not in the second. Thus the American flag, which Tillich would say is a symbol of the American nation, may *function* as a symbol and as a sign. For most Americans it undoubtedly functions as a symbol. But to school children of another country engaged in the task of learning the flags of the various nations, it may function only as a sign. In calling *x* a *symbol,* what must be meant, on Tillich's theory, is that *x* functions as a symbol for some group. *X* is a *live* symbol only if it functions as a symbol for some presently existing group. If there once was such a group, but no such group presently exists, then *x* is a *dead* symbol. The story of religion is largely, for Tillich, the story of the birth and death of religious symbols.

In this chapter I have endeavored to explain and critically evaluate the various, and often insightful, claims Tillich makes concerning signs and symbols. Some of these claims—for example, the claim that symbols, but not signs, participate in that to which they point—were rejected for various reasons. Other claims seemed clear and plausible enough to be useful in explicating Tillich's concept of a sign and his concept of a symbol. In explaining and evaluating Tillich's views concerning signs, I discussed linguistic, as well as non-linguistic, signs. However, in examining his notion of a symbol I focussed almost entirely on non-linguistic symbols. Linguistic symbols, I believe, present special difficulties. Some of these difficulties will emerge in our examination of Tillich's views concerning the nature of religious symbols and myths. No discussion of religious symbols can avoid an examination of religious discourse since, as Tillich rightly maintains, religious language is incurably symbolic.

V

The Nature of the Religious Symbol

IN CHAPTER I we noted that Tillich's identification of God with being-itself may be viewed as an attempt to provide a doctrine of God which adequately accounts for a basic tension in the religious idea of God—a tension between what he speaks of as "a tendency toward ultimacy" and "a tendency toward concreteness." Since being-itself is beyond all limitations, it is not difficult to see how the identification of God with being-itself satisfies the tendency toward ultimacy in the idea of God. But on the surface it would appear that the identification of God with being-itself renders it impossible to accommodate the tendency toward concreteness, a tendency that is reflected both in the religious man's conception of God and in his experience of God. For, as Tillich readily acknowledges, God is conceived by the religious man as a more or less *concrete being*—Yahweh, Baal, Zeus, Odin, etc.—and, moreover, experienced as *personal*. How then can these religious facts be accounted for within a theological system which identifies God with that which is not even *a* being, let alone a *personal* being? Once God is identified with the ultimate of Tillich's ontology, being-itself, how is it possible to account for the tendency toward concreteness in the idea of God? The clearest expression by Tillich of the difficulty this question raises is the following:

Is not God in the religious encounter *a* person among others, related to them as an *I* to a *thou*, and vice versa? And, if so, is he not *a* being, while the ontological question asks the question of being-itself, of the power of being in and above all beings? In the ontological question, is not God himself transcended? (BR, 27–28).

The burden of Tillich's attempt to resolve the difficulty expressed in the paragraph above rests on his theory of religious symbols. It is the religious symbol vis-à-vis its intimate relation to being-itself which, on Tillich's theory, accommodates the tendency toward concreteness in the religious conception and experience of God. In brief, his view is that by virtue of the participation of every being in being-itself every being has the potential to express the concrete element in the idea and experience of God. Any being which actually expresses this element is, for Tillich, a religious symbol.

My purpose in this chapter and the next is to explicate and examine Tillich's theory of religious symbols considering the extent to which his theory provides a coherent and adequate account of the concrete element in the idea and experience of God. Of course, any difficulties inherent in the theory as such will affect its adequacy to accommodate the tendency toward concreteness.

Religious symbols—both linguistic and non-linguistic—must share the basic features which, for Tillich, distinguish the class of symbols from the class of signs. But, as Tillich realizes, more must be said if we are to understand the nature of the religious symbol, what it is for something to be a religious symbol. Specifically, we must come to understand precisely what differentiates religious symbols from non-religious symbols—political, artistic, historical, etc.

In discussing what distinguishes the religious from the non-religious symbol Tillich remarks:

> The religious symbol has a special character in that it points to the ultimate level of being, to ultimate reality, to being-itself, to meaning itself. That which is the ground of being is the object to which the religious symbol points. It points to that which is of ultimate concern for us, to that which is infinitely meaningful and unconditionally valid. Religious experience is the experience of that which concerns us ultimately. The content of this experience is expressed in religious symbols.[1]

In this statement two interesting points are made: religious symbols point to being-itself; and being-itself is that which is of ultimate concern for us. Tillich also suggests that religious symbols "express" the *content* of the experience of ultimate concern. Elsewhere he makes it clear that in the experience of ultimate concern there is always a more or less 'concrete' content and that religious symbols—presumably non-linguistic religious symbols—are in fact identical with this concrete content. Thus, after noting that there is absolute certainty regarding the experience of ultimacy as such when one is ultimately concerned, he says, "But there is not certainty of this kind about the *content* of our ultimate concern, be it nation, success, a god, or the God of the Bible: They all are contents without immediate awareness" (DF, 17). Again he remarks: "It is not risk and needs no courage with respect to ultimacy itself. But it is risk and demands courage if it affirms a concrete concern. And every faith has a concrete element in itself. It is concerned about something or somebody" (DF, 18). These remarks

---

[1] Paul Tillich, "Theology and Symbolism," *Religious Symbolism*, ed. F. Earnest Johnson (New York: Harper & Brothers, 1955), pp. 109–10.

imply that in the experience of ultimate concern the concern is directed to the ultimate (being-itself) via some concrete content (a religious symbol). Hence, these remarks entitle us to add a third point to the two cited above. The three points together are: (1) religious symbols point to being-itself, (2) being-itself is that which is of ultimate concern for us, and (3) the concrete content of our ultimate concern is a religious symbol.

In the first chapter I discussed point 2 and suggested the metaphysical line of reasoning which leads Tillich to the conclusion there expressed. Points 1 and 3 seem to suggest two ways of distinguishing religious symbols from non-religious symbols. The first, based on 1, I shall call, for want of a better term, the *objective way* of distinguishing the religious symbol. The second, based on 3, I shall call the *subjective way* of distinguishing religious from non-religious symbols. The objective way distinguishes the religious symbol in terms of its objective referent, what it points to. The subjective way differentiates the religious symbol in terms of the way in which it is experienced; it is the focus of ultimate concern. Each of these must be discussed in detail.

We have seen that Tillich is concerned to assert the reality of being-itself and yet to deny that it is an existing object in the world, existing alongside of other objects. It is this character of being-itself—that it is real but is not an existing object among other objects—that Tillich is relying on in suggesting that the religious symbol can be adequately distinguished from other symbols by virtue of the fact that it points to being-itself. If we find a symbol which points to some existing object in the world, it follows from what Tillich has said that that symbol is not a religious symbol. Thus the flag may symbolize the king or the political state, but the king and the state have objective existence in the world. Hence, the flag is not a religious symbol since that to which the religious symbol points is not an existing object in the world. But will this do? Are there not some admittedly secular symbols which do not point to existing objects in the world? And are there not some admittedly religious symbols (e.g., the crucifix) which do point to events in history or definite objects? Concerning the crucifix Tillich makes the following interesting comment: "Devotion to the crucifix is really directed to the crucifixion on Golgotha and devotion to the latter is in reality intended for the redemptive action of God, which is itself a symbolic expression for an experience of what concerns us ultimately."[2] Presumably, Tillich would say, in answer to the second question, that a religious symbol points either to being-itself or to existing events or objects which themselves are symbols pointing to being-itself—that is, a religious symbol points to being-itself either directly or indirectly. One could say that first-order religious symbols point to being-itself, second-order religious symbols point to first-order ones, n-order religious symbols point to $n - 1$ order religious symbols. In this way Tillich can resolve the problem raised by the second question asked above.

To the first question concerning admittedly secular symbols which are not taken as pointing to existing objects in the world, Tillich remarks:

---

[2] Paul Tillich, "The Religious Symbol," *Religious Experience and Truth*, ed. Sidney Hook (New York: New York University Press, 1961), p. 301. This essay is mainly a reprint of an article by the same title which appeared in the summer issue of *The Journal of Liberal Religion*, 1940.

All other symbols either stand for something that has also an un-symbolic objective existence aside from its ideal significance, as, for example, a flag can represent a king, and the king in turn represents the state; or they are the forms giving expression to an invisible thing that has no existence except in its symbols, as for example, cultural creations like works of art, scientific concepts, and legal forms. It is only in symbolic fashion that such intangible things as these can be given expression at all.[3]

The point here is obscure. Either Tillich means to be saying that what these symbols—other than the flag, etc.—point to has no ontological status at all—whereas being-itself does—or, more likely, he is saying that although what they point to does not exist as an object in the world, it, nevertheless, is a thing or an aspect of reality, and to that extent conditioned, limited. I am inclined toward the second of these alternatives as being the correct interpretation of this passage. If this is so, we can put Tillich's distinction more simply by saying that whereas non-religious symbols point to levels of reality which are limited or conditioned, the religious symbol points to the absolutely unconditioned level which is presupposed by all other levels. He sometimes draws the distinction in this way.

Religious symbols do exactly the same thing as all symbols do—namely, they open up a level of reality which otherwise is not opened at all, which is hidden. We can call this the depth dimension of reality itself, the dimension of reality which is the ground of every other dimension and every other depth, and which therefore, is not one level beside the others but is the fundamental level, the level below all other levels, the level of being-itself, or the ultimate power of being (TC, 58–59).

Suppose that, in spite of the difficulties raised in earlier chapters, we adopt the view that reality is not composed entirely of particular beings, but includes and at the ulti-

---

[3] Tillich, *Religious Experience and Truth,* p. 303.

mate level is identical with something which is absolutely unconditioned; namely, being-itself. On this supposition, Tillich's claim is that the religious symbol, as distinguished from the non-religious symbol, points to being-itself. But how are we to understand the assertion that religious symbols *point to* being-itself? In the previous chapter I argued that the most plausible interpretation of 'points to' is *signifies.* Moreover, where x is a symbol of y for S the relation of signification in which x stands to y is, I suggested, either the result of a conscious decision (e.g., the recent decision by which a new flag was made to signify the Canadian nation) and gains unconscious acceptance *or* the result of unconscious processes (e.g., the child who is unaware that a doll functions for her as a symbol of her mother). Now assuming that x is a symbol for S (a group or person), and that our partial analysis of Tillich's concept of a symbol— presented in the previous chapter—is correct, it follows that x signifies being-itself for S. The question we must ask is: What sense can be made out of the claim that x signifies being-itself for S?

Can it be that those for whom x is a religious symbol *consciously decide* that x shall signify being-itself, and then accept and respond to this signification on the unconscious level? The difficulty with an affirmative answer to this question is that it seems to presuppose that those who consciously decide have some concept of that which they are taking x to signify; that is, that they have some concept of being-itself. Indeed, it seems quite impossible that someone should *consciously decide* to let x signify y and yet have no concept of y. One could not decide that four bells are to signify fire unless one had a concept of fire. But, quite likely, most religious people for whom certain objects are religious symbols have no concept of being-itself. Hence, if we are to say that these religious symbols signify being-itself, we cannot understand this as implying that religious men have *consciously decided* to let these objects signify being-itself.

In his excellent essay "Tillich's Conception of a Religious Symbol," Alston develops the difficulty noted above into a much stronger objection. He argues that for x to function as a symbol of y for S, S *must* be able to *specify y* as that which is being symbolized. Unless S could do this, ". . . we would be hard pressed to give any sense to saying that the object was taken to represent anything other than itself; it would simply be an effective stimulus for certain emotional states."[4] "I am not, indeed, asserting that every time a person responds to x as a religious symbol, he tells himself what it is this object symbolizes. But I am saying that he would be capable of specifying the symbolizandum on demand."[5] If Alston is right about this it seems very unlikely that religious symbols point to (signify) being-itself for ordinary religious people. For, as Alston observes:

> . . . it would seem that one could *specify* being-itself as what certain symbols point to only if he went through something like the ontological discussion Tillich goes through in introducing the concept. But that would mean that religious symbols function as such only for metaphysicians, indeed, only for metaphysicians of a certain stripe—a conclusion which would surely be as abhorrent to Tillich as to anyone else.[6]

Undoubtedly, Alston's objection is a forceful one. Indeed, if it is correct a rather fundamental claim in Tillich's theory of religious symbols—namely, that religious symbols

---

[4] Alston, *Religious Experience and Truth,* p. 13.

[5] *Ibid.*   [6] *Ibid.*, p. 18.

point to being-itself—is shown to be false. Moreover, on the face of it, Alston's objection appears sound. Surely I could hardly say that the weeping willow is a symbol for me unless I could specify or indicate what it symbolizes, say, unhappy love. But perhaps we are moving too quickly here. There indeed may be something wrong or odd in *my* saying that x is a symbol for me, and then admitting that I do not have a clue as to what it symbolizes for me. (Compare, "I believe that Jones will not come, but he will come.")[7] Whereas there may not be anything wrong or odd in someone else saying of *me* that x functions as a symbol for me, although I do not know and, hence, cannot specify what it is that x symbolizes for me. (Compare, "Smith believes that Jones will not come, but he will.")

Consider the following statement forms: (a) x functions as a symbol of y for S; (b) S is unable to specify what x symbolizes. If Tillich is to maintain that religious symbols symbolize being-itself, then I believe he must hold that at least some substitutions for statement form (a) are not incompatible with the corresponding substitutions for the statement form b. Alston's remarks imply that (a) and (b) are incompatible statement forms. That is, Alston holds that unless S can specify what x symbolizes, x *cannot* function as a symbol for S. On this issue Alston is, I believe, mistaken. Suppose, to expand an example introduced earlier, that a young child who is unnaturally preoccupied with a particular doll is brought to a psychotherapist for treatment. After several interviews the psychotherapist writes in his notebook that the doll functions as a symbol

---

[7] Actually, this comparison is too strong. I suggest below a set of circumstances in which I might say that something functions as a symbol for me, admitting that I do not know what it symbolizes.

for the child of her mother, that the child is unaware of this and, hence, quite unable to specify what the doll symbolizes. Indeed, it *might* happen that on the authority of the therapist the child comes to believe that the doll is a symbol for something else, and yet still be ignorant of the fact that the doll symbolizes her mother. Thus even though the child *cannot specify* what the doll symbolizes, the doll may nevertheless be a symbol for her of her mother, and the psychotherapist may truthfully record this fact. Finally, we can imagine a point at which the child might *realize* that the doll is a symbol for her and yet still be unable to determine just what in her emotional environment it symbolizes.[8] I conclude from this case that x may function as a symbol of y for S even though S is unable to specify what x symbolizes.

The inability of religious men to specify being-itself as that which their sacred objects signify or point to does not, I believe, imply that these religious objects do not function as symbols for being-itself. It does, however, show rather conclusively that the relationship of signification in which these religious objects stand to being-itself is not the result of *conscious decision.* Otherwise, we should expect those for whom these objects are religious symbols to be able to specify what it is that they are symbols of. That is, *if* religious symbols do signify being-itself, the relation of signifi-

---

[8] Certain analogies between the child-therapist example and the relationship between the plain religious man and Tillich suggest themselves. Just as the doll may function as a symbol even though the patient is unaware of its symbolic character so may the traditional image of God as the supreme being function as a symbol even though the plain religious man is unaware of its symbolic character. Just as the therapist with his knowledge and skill can discover what the symbol stands for so may the philosophical theologian discover what is symbolized by the plain religious man's image of God, etc.

cation between them does not result from conscious decision in the way in which the relation of signification between, say, the swastika and the Nazi movement was the result of the conscious decision of Hitler or his underlings.

In discussing Tillich's concept of a symbol in the previous chapter I noted that a crucial feature of his view is that symbols emerge when there is an unconscious need for them, and that the relationship of signification between x and y, even if established by conscious decision, must gain unconscious acceptance and fulfill some deep unconscious need in order for x to be a symbol. We also observed that the relation of signification between x and y may itself be established on the level of the unconscious. It now appears that in so far as a religious symbol signifies (points to) being-itself this relation of signification is due wholly to unconscious needs. Tillich's view as to what these needs are has been sketched in earlier chapters—man's existential anxiety, his need to come into vital contact with that reality which transcends the threat of nonbeing, etc.

There are, it seems to me, two questions that must be carefully distinguished in discussing the objective way for distinguishing religious from non-religious symbols. The first question is whether we can use the fact—assuming for the moment that it is a fact—that religious symbols point to being-itself as a way of determining whether a given symbol is a religious symbol or not. That is, does the objective way provide us with an *effective criterion* for separating out the class of religious symbols? Assuming that we are compelled to answer the first question in the negative, the second question is whether it is, nevertheless, a truth about religious symbols that they do point, whether directly or indirectly, to being-itself. It would be a mistake to think that a negative answer to the first question requires a negative answer to the second.

That the objective way does not provide us with an effective tool for selecting from the class of symbols those which are religious symbols can be shown by the following considerations. Suppose (1) that 'being-itself' designates something real that is absolutely unconditioned and (2) that the religious symbol, unlike other symbols, points to being-itself—either directly or indirectly. The question we need to ask is whether, supposing 1 and 2 to be true, we are in any better position than if they were not true (*a*) to identify x as a religious symbol, or (*b*) given the information that x, y, and z are symbols, to be able to single out x as a religious symbol. Let us consider *b* first. It is perhaps true that, assuming 1 and 2, we could decide certain cases as *not* being religious symbols. That is, if z, say, is a flag and evokes feelings of patriotism for one's country, etc., we could, given 1 and 2, be fairly sure that z is not a religious symbol, for the flag would be recognized as referring to or pointing to the nation—and we know that religious symbols do not point to such objects. This assumes, of course, that the nation does not point to being-itself—in which case the flag might point indirectly to being-itself—and that a symbol cannot point directly to more than one entity. But, whereas in the case of z we can discover its relation to the nation, there is no corresponding way in which we can discover that x refers to being-itself. For, although we can determine the way we respond to the nation *independently* of the way we respond to the flag, there is no way of determining our reaction to being-itself independent of our reactions to some religious symbol, because Tillich holds that being-itself cannot be encountered directly, only through symbols.[9] Hence, even if we know that x is a symbol, 1 and 2 do not enable us to identify it as a religious symbol. If 1 and 2 are insufficient to perform b—to identify a symbol as a religious symbol—it is clear that they are also insufficient to identify x, when we do not already know that it is a symbol, as a religious symbol. It appears then that the *objective way* is not a way at all, it is a criterion neither for identifying something as a religious symbol nor for identifying a symbol as a religious symbol. However, the point Tillich is endeavoring to make must not be dismissed prematurely. It may be that religious symbols do perform the function of pointing to being-itself, a function not performed by non-religious symbols. All that we have shown is that this fact would not enable us to distinguish in practice between religious and non-religious symbols.

The subjective way of distinguishing religious symbols from non-religious symbols rests on the claim that only the former are the foci of ultimate concern. This, I think, is the criterion Tillich actually uses in identifying something as a religious symbol. This means that for x to be a religious symbol it must be the focus of ultimate concern. Being the focus of ultimate concern is a necessary and sufficient condition for x being a religious symbol. What I am suggesting here is that in practice, Tillich's way of distinguishing religious symbols from other kinds of symbols rests upon the place that the symbol occupies in the psychic life of the individual or group. To say of an object that it is a "religious symbol" or "sacred object" is not to ascribe an objective property to that object; a property which, like weight

---

[9] This point was first noted by Alston in "Tillich on Idolatry," *The Journal of Religion*, 38 (October, 1958): 263–67.

or shape, the object has independently of the way in which men feel toward and respond to the object. Rather it is to say that the object is the focus of a particular attitude, the religious attitude, which Tillich speaks of as 'ultimate concern'.

Perhaps the following suggestion concerning the structure of Tillich's thought will help illuminate his concept of a religious symbol. In terms of the logical development—not necessarily temporal development—of his thought we can picture Tillich as beginning with what anyone would regard as a clear case of a group's relation to a sacred object of worship. The object—say, Buddha or Christ—is, Tillich notes, experienced as holy, the focus of feelings of awe and mystery, the center of life and meaning for the group. Tillich introduces the expression 'ultimate concern' to stand for this complex of attitudes and feelings directed at these admittedly sacred objects. The concept of ultimate concern then takes on a fundamental role in his thought. It becomes, for Tillich, the primary and definitive notion in religion. Wherever there is ultimate concern—directed at no matter what—religion is present. Without ultimate concern there is no religion. If we think of religion as a complex activity involving not only feelings and attitudes, but beliefs, creeds, institutions, etc., we must, I think, regard Tillich as signaling out the *subjective element*—feelings and attitudes—and attaching primary importance to that element, making it definitive of religion itself. Tillich, like Schleiermacher before him, regards a certain feeling or attitude, ultimate concern, as the *definitive* element in religion. This leads Tillich to the view that religion exceeds its own boundaries. By this paradoxical remark I mean simply that having made *ultimate concern* the definitive element in religion, Tillich is led to extend the term 'religion' to activities and forms of life not normally called 'religions' but, nevertheless, ones in which ultimate concern—the subjective element in religion—is to be found. In his later writings this point is made admirably clear. Thus, while in dialogue with students, Tillich remarked:

If religion is defined as a state of 'being grasped by an ultimate concern'—which is also my definition of faith—then we must distinguish this as a universal or large concept from our usual smaller concept of religion which supposes an organized group with its clergy, scriptures, and dogma, by which a set of symbols for the ultimate concern is accepted and cultivated in life and thought. This is religion in the narrower sense of the word, while religion defined *as* 'ultimate concern' is religion in the larger sense of the word.

This is why in my little book *Christianity and the Encounter of the World Religions* I have discussed the concept of quasi-religions—ideologies, such as nationalism or socialism, which claim the loyalty or veneration of their followers with the intensity sometimes of the theistic religions. This term 'quasi-religion' would be meaningless if we defined religion solely in the smaller, narrower sense of the word. But in the light of the larger concept we can understand that ultimate concern is also present in what we usually call the secular or profane.[10]

Just as the primacy of the concept of ultimate concern leads Tillich to extend the terms 'religion' and 'religious' beyond their normal uses, Tillich is led to extend the expression 'religious symbol' to objects not normally thought to be either religious or symbolic. However, the matter is a good deal more complicated. Not only are entities, goals, etc., that are not normally thought to be religious symbols or sacred objects—e.g., success, one's nation, etc.,—called 'religious symbols' by Tillich when they become the foci of

---

[10] *Ultimate Concern: Tillich in Dialogue,* ed. D. Mackenzie Brown (New York: Harper & Row, Publishers, 1965), pp. 4–5. Hereafter references to this work will appear in the text abbreviated as UC.

ultimate concern, but within the context of religion itself Tillich speaks of some entities as religious symbols which traditionally have not been thought to be symbols at all. For example, the theistic God of the Judaic-Christian tradition is held by Tillich to be a religious symbol. "The fundamental symbol of our ultimate concern is God" (DF, 45). Within the Judaic-Christian tradition various objects and events have been taken as symbolic of God's nature and activities. But God himself as the supremely perfect being has not been taken as a symbol—at least not generally.

I have suggested that the criterion by which Tillich determines the class of religious symbols is the subjective way. Whatever *object*, remembering that being-itself is not an object, is the focus of ultimate concern is a religious symbol. Of course, Tillich maintains that religious symbols, like all symbols, point to something else. Moreover, unlike other symbols, religious symbols point to being-itself. But this latter claim, I am suggesting, does not have the status of a criterion for determining what is a religious symbol and what is not. Rather, once we have determined—by the subjective way—what entities are religious symbols, the objective way may be construed as an attempt by Tillich to offer an ontological explanation for the phenomenological fact that ultimate concern is directed at these entities. By claiming that religious symbols point to being-itself Tillich endeavors both to explain why men direct ultimate concern toward finite objects, religious symbols, and to avoid rendering religion entirely subjective.

In both Chapter I and Chapter IV, we saw that it is important to distinguish (1) Tillich's phenomenological description of religious experience and (2) the elaborate ontology that he employs in explaining the phenomena of religious experience and ultimate concern. These two aspects of his philosophical theology are woven together in his writings; only infrequently does the distinction come to the surface. One point at which it does emerge explicitly is in his discussion of the question: What is the referent of religious symbolism? On the one hand we have his penetrating description of religious and quasi-religious experience—a description of ultimate concern directed at various finite ends and objects. On the other hand we have his ontological analysis of man's situation in the world, his anxiety occasioned by the threat of nonbeing, his longing for being-itself, for some vital contact with that reality which possesses the power of overcoming the threat of nonbeing. He endeavors to connect the description of religious experience with his neo-Platonic ontology in his concept of the religious symbol. Ultimate concern and being-itself merge in the religious symbol. As we have noted, a religious symbol is any *object* (I use 'object' here to cover not only physical objects, such as people and statues, but also institutions and goals) which is the focus of ultimate concern. In arguing for the claim that religious symbols point to being-itself Tillich explicitly distinguishes between an *ontological approach,* described above, and a *phenomenological approach.* Thus, in discussing the problem of determining the referent of religious symbolism, he remarks, "There are two ways which lead to the same result, a phenomenological and an ontological one."[11] It is important to our understanding Tillich's view of religious symbols to undertake some account of his attempt to intro-

---

11 Tillich, "The Meaning and Justification of Religious Symbols," *Religious Experience and Truth,* p. 6.

duce being-itself as the referent of religious symbols by the phenomenological approach.

Tillich's statement of the phenomenological way of showing that being-itself is the referent of the religious symbol is as follows:

> The phenomenological approach describes the holy as a quality of some encounters with reality. The holy is a "quality in encounter," not an object among objects, and not an emotional response without a basis in the whole of objects. The experience of the holy transcends the subject-object structure of experience. The subject is drawn into the holy, embodied in a finite object which, in this encounter, becomes sacred. An analysis of this experience shows that wherever the holy appears it is a matter of ultimate concern both in attracting and in repelling, and of unconditional power, both in giving and demanding.[12]

Perhaps some clarification of these remarks can be attained by considering an example or two. In the religious act man is ultimately concerned. Something concrete—a statue, a nation, Christ—becomes the content of his ultimate concern. Let us consider the case in which the concrete content of ultimate concern is a nation. What we need to recognize here is that when the nation—or anything else, for that matter—becomes the content of one's ultimate concern the nation *as an object of experience* is vastly transformed. It is experienced as having qualities which transcend the ordinary properties of nations. One consequence of this phenomenological fact is that the nation can no longer be described completely and satisfactorily in nonsymbolic language. This, perhaps, comes as something of a surprise. It is one thing to maintain that being-itself, the referent of the religious symbol, requires symbolic language for its description. It is quite another thing to claim

---

12 *Ibid.*

that the symbol itself requires symbolic language for its description. But unless I seriously misunderstand Tillich, his view is that the religious symbol—in this example the nation itself—also requires symbolic language. Thus Tillich claims that "man's ultimate concern must be expressed symbolically" (DF, 44). But if the content of a man's ultimate concern is his nation, one can reasonably ask why this is so. For do we not often speak about the nation in non-symbolic language? Surely, we do, and if the nation is the content of our ultimate concern, is it not a mistake to say that it requires symbolic language for its expression?

If money, success or the nation is someone's ultimate concern, can this not be said in a direct way without symbolic language? Is it not only in those cases in which the content of the ultimate concern is called "God" that we are in the realm of symbols? The answer is that everything which is a matter of unconditional concern is made into a god. If the nation is someone's ultimate concern, the name of the nation becomes a sacred name and the nation receives divine qualities which far surpass the reality of the being and functioning of the nation. The nation then stands for and symbolizes the true ultimate, but in an idolatrous way (DF, 44).

Ignoring until the last chapter Tillich's reference to idolatry, what I think is being maintained in this and other passages is that the nation as a political, physical reality is transformed and transcended when it becomes the content of the experience of ultimate concern. In experiencing the nation with ultimate concern one experiences it as holy, as exhibiting a quality which is unconditioned, transcending the realm of the finite. Thus to experience the nation as *holy* —and whatever is the content of ultimate concern is experienced *as holy*—is to experience the nation as exhibiting a quality which is unique and indescribable in nonsymbolic language. And it is because the nation is experienced as *holy,* as exhibiting this indescribable quality, that Tillich maintains that the nation *as the content of ultimate concern* cannot be described or even named without the employment of symbolic language. It is important to note that 'the holy' designates a unique *quality,* not an object. Tillich says, "The holy is a 'quality in encounter,' not an object among objects, . . ." This quality is exhibited by the finite object which is the content of ultimate concern. Thus Tillich says, "The subject is drawn into the holy, embodied in a finite object which, in the encounter, becomes sacred." Again, it is *because* the object which is the content of ultimate concern "embodies" this unique, indescribable quality that it requires symbolic language for its description.

Tillich acknowledges his indebtedness to Rudolf Otto's penetrating phenomenological analysis of the experience of the holy. In *The Idea of the Holy,* Otto argued that religious experience presents us with something that is indescribable and unique. "For if there be any single domain of human experience that presents us with something unmistakably specific and unique, peculiar to itself, assuredly it is that of the religious life."[13] Otto uses the expression "the holy" to designate this unique element, an element which can only be spoken of symbolically for it "remains inexpressible—an ἄρρητον or *ineffabile*—in the sense that it completely eludes apprehension in terms of concepts."[14] Tillich accepts Otto's phenomenological analysis of the holy, identifying the holy with a unique and indescribable quality embodied in the objects which form the concrete content of the experience of ultimate concern.

---

[13] Rudolf Otto, *The Idea of the Holy* (New York: Oxford University Press, 1923), p. 4.

[14] *Ibid.,* p. 5.

We have seen that ultimate concern is, apparently, always directed at some concrete content—the religious symbol. Moreover, and perhaps more importantly, we have noted that in the experience of ultimate concern the concrete content is transformed and transcended; it embodies and manifests a unique, indescribable quality, *the holy.* Finally, we noted that a consequence of this transformation is that the concrete content—the religious symbol—as experienced requires symbolic language for its description. Thus, the religious symbol *itself,* not just its referent, must be described in symbolic language. But, if I interpret Tillich correctly, this is because of the *way* in which the religious symbol—in our example, the nation—is connected with its referent, *the holy.* The holy is a quality *embodied in* the concrete content or religious symbol. Hence, the necessity of symbolic language in speaking about the religious symbol is due to the intimate connection that exists between the religious symbol and its referent; namely, the holy.

But several questions remain. Does everyone have an ultimate concern? Does every ultimate concern involve some concrete content? Or, can the holy be experienced independently of any symbol, any concrete content? And, finally, can the phenomenological approach establish the objective validity of the holy? That is, on the assumption that being-itself is the metaphysical ultimate, can the phenomenological approach justify the conclusion that the ultimate encountered in religious experience is the *ontological ultimate,* being-itself? Perhaps the best strategy for deepening our understanding of Tillich's theory of religious symbols is to discuss each of these questions in turn.

After reading Otto's penetrating phenomenological analysis of the experience of the holy, and Tillich's discussion of what is involved in being ultimately concerned about some object—remembering that it is, in part, to experience the object as holy—one is apt to feel that most men are born and die without ever being grasped by an ultimate concern, without ever experiencing anything as *holy,* in Otto's sense of that term. Perhaps the mystics and other men of high religious genius are grasped by an ultimate concern and, consequently, encounter the holy; but ordinary men, religious and non-religious, seem not to undergo such an experience. Perhaps during the early Hitler period some Nazis became, as Tillich believes, ultimately concerned about the German nation. But surely for most men the nation is not an object of ultimate concern. Perhaps some Christians and Buddhists are ultimately concerned about Christ and Buddha respectively, but surely many adherents to these religious traditions never *experience* the unique, indescribable quality of the holy as embodied in these sacred objects. Indeed, Tillich seems aware of this fact when he speaks of the decline and death of symbols, of their failing to evoke in men the response of ultimate concern which they once evoked. Hence, one is surprised to learn that Tillich holds that *everyone* has an ultimate concern, that everyone is grasped by the holy. Thus, speaking of the experience of ultimate concern, Tillich remarks:

And my thesis is that everybody experiences it at some time or place, although often it is hard to discover, for oneself or for others. But it is my experience that among all the human beings I have ever met—quite a few!—I have never found anybody who had nothing which he took with unconditional seriousness. There was always something. The ultimate experiment, perhaps, is to find out from the cynic who says to you, "I don't take anything seriously," what he actually does take seriously; sometimes it is his glory in cynicism, or possibly his despair in it. Since I know this qualitatively different concern in myself, I can perhaps see it or recognize it also in others. If one has never recognized it in oneself, even though it is there, it is hard to recognize in others (UC, 27–28).

Why should Tillich burden himself with the *implausible* thesis that everyone has an ultimate concern? Surely not because of the empirical fact—if it is a fact—that he has found most or all of his acquaintances to have an ultimate concern. For to claim that everyone has an ultimate concern is to imply that everyone has *an awareness of the holy*. As Tillich says, where there is faith—he defines 'faith' as the state of being ultimately concerned—"there is awareness of holiness" (DF, 12). What drives him to maintain the extreme thesis that everyone has an ultimate concern is, I believe, not empirical data but a certain line of metaphysical reasoning to the effect that since every man is exposed to the ontological threat of nonbeing, every man is ultimately concerned about that reality which can overcome this ontological threat, namely, being-itself. And if the metaphysical reasoning leads to a conclusion that seems to conflict with the empirical data, then so much the worse for the data. True, Tillich endeavors to neutralize the fact that many are honestly unaware of ever experiencing the holy by the suggestion that one's ultimate concern may be unconscious. But I find it almost as difficult to conceive of someone having an experience of the ultimate and not being *aware* of it as to conceive of someone experiencing a sharp pain and being unaware of the pain. I am afraid that in suggesting that someone may have an ultimate concern and yet not recognize it or be aware of it, Tillich forgets how much he has *built into* the concept of ultimate concern—an ever present danger when one takes an ordinary expression like 'concern' and uses it in a technical sense when qualified by the adjective 'ultimate'. Of course someone can fail to recognize just how serious he is about gaining success, or just how concerned he really is about someone or something. But to be *ultimately concerned* about *x* is not just to be very concerned about *x;* it is, in part, to *experience x as holy,* as embodying a unique, indescribable quality of ultimacy. Tillich simply does not explain how one can experience *x* in that way without recognizing that he has done so. The fact that someone is unable to single out *anything* that he has *experienced* in that way is, I should think, *prima facie* evidence, at the very least, that he has experienced nothing in that way. To say that he may, nevertheless, be very, very serious about *x* without realizing it and to conclude that he, therefore, may be ultimately concerned about *x* after all, is either to engage in fallacious reasoning or to equivocate on the expression 'ultimate concern'.

In Chapter I we noted Tillich's claim that ". . . it is impossible to be concerned about something which cannot be encountered *concretely,* be it in the realm of reality or in the realm of the imagination. . . ." (ST, 1:211. Italics mine.) This claim certainly implies an affirmative answer to our second question raised above: Does every ultimate concern involve some concrete content? That his answer is affirmative is also clearly implied in the following two remarks:

There is no faith without a content toward which it is directed. There is always something meant in the act of faith (DF, 10).

Ultimate concern is ultimate risk and ultimate courage. It is not risk and needs no courage with respect to ultimacy itself. But it is risk and demands courage if it affirms a concrete concern. And every faith has a concrete element in itself. It is concerned about something or somebody (DF, 18).

However, after saying in *Dynamics of Faith* (p. 18) that every faith (ultimate concern) has a concrete content, Tillich contradicts himself when he remarks: "The skeptic, so long as he is a serious skeptic, is not without faith, even though it has no concrete content" (DF, 20). But clearly his predominant view is that every ultimate concern has a concrete content, that every experience of the holy is an experience of the holy *as embodied* in this or that concrete object. Indeed, I argued in Chapter I that only if ultimate concern has some concrete content as its focus can we make sense out of Tillich's view that that which is our ultimate concern demands total surrender and promises total fulfillment. It makes sense, for example, to speak of someone's being totally committed to a person (Christ, Napoleon, etc.) or a political movement (communism, fascism, etc.), but what sense does it make to speak of someone's being totally committed to being-itself. Thus in view of what Tillich packs into his concept of ultimate concern it is necessary, I believe, for him to hold, as he apparently does, that every ultimate concern has a concrete content.

There is one difficulty with Tillich's claim that every ultimate concern has a concrete content that requires some discussion. So far as I can determine Tillich nowhere explains what he means by the expression 'concrete content'. Why is this a difficulty? It is a difficulty because, unless we understand what he means by 'concrete content,' we have no way of knowing what is being included and what is being excluded from the role of being an object of ultimate concern. One is apt to think, for example, that to be 'concrete' the content of one's concern must be some object that either does exist or at one time did exist—a statue, a tree, a historical figure (Christ, Buddha, etc.). But, as we have seen, the content of one's concern may not be a physical object at all; it may be an institution (the state), a political movement (communism), a goal (success), an historical event (the crucifixion). Indeed, if I understand Tillich correctly, it may even be a non-existing, purely imaginary being. Thus the God of traditional theism who is a supremely perfect being, creator of the natural world and man, etc., is the concrete content of the ultimate concern of many Christians. But, as a matter of fact, reality, according to Tillich, does not contain such a being. Zeus, Baal, Odin, Yahweh, and the God of traditional theism are *imaginary* beings. No list of the existing beings that make up the furniture of the universe would include these 'beings'. However, for Tillich they are excellent examples, nevertheless, of religious symbols, of concrete contents of ultimate concern. Even *abstract* ideals and ideas (humanism, socialism, etc.) may be the foci of ultimate concern (UC, 29). In fact, it would seem that Tillich is prepared to count anything whatever—existing or nonexisting—short of being-itself as a candidate for inclusion within the scope of the expression "the concrete content of ultimate concern." But if something quite *abstract* (the natural opposite of 'concrete') can be the concrete content of ultimate concern, the word 'concrete' has been taken from its natural environment and given a technical meaning within Tillich's system. Moreover, the difficulties we encountered in trying to explicate Tillich's concept of being-itself confront us again. For 'concrete content' now seems to mean simply *anything other than being-itself*. But even though the intension of 'concrete content' is unclear—owing to the conceptual unclarity of 'being-itself'—perhaps we have a sufficient list of examples from its extension to provide at least some understanding of the expression as it is used by Tillich.

The final question we must raise concerning the phenomenological approach to determining the referent of religious symbolism is: Can the phenomenological approach establish the objective validity of the holy? The question presupposes Tillich's view that being-itself is what is ontologically ultimate. On this assumption it asks whether the phenomenological approach can establish that *the holy,* a unique quality of ultimacy experienced as embodied in the concrete content (religious symbol) of ultimate concern, is in fact the *ontological ultimate,* being-itself? This is a question of considerable importance, the answer to which, although negative, requires careful consideration in order to be properly understood. Tillich's remark that bears most directly on our question is the following:

The phenomenological analysis of the experience of the holy has been carried through in an excellent way by Rudolf Otto and others. It shows what is meant, if religious symbols are used. But it cannot go beyond the description. Phenomenology cannot raise the question of validity of the phenomena it makes visible.[15]

At the risk of misinterpreting Tillich's appraisal of the phenomenological approach I wish to suggest, as a beginning, that our question is complex. Prior to raising the question whether the holy is identical with being-itself, we must ask whether the holy is *subjective* or *objective.* Only if the holy is in some sense objective can we go on to ask whether it is in fact the ontological ultimate, being-itself. For, however unclear we may be about Tillich's con-

---

[15] Tillich, "The Meaning and Justification of Religious Symbols," *Religious Experience and Truth,* p. 7.

cept of being-itself, we can at least be sure that he does not mean by it any thing or quality that is merely *subjective*. Hence, our prior question must be: Can the phenomenological approach establish that the holy is not simply a purely subjective quality within the experience of ultimate concern. But the expressions 'subjective' and 'objective' are themselves notoriously unclear. Hence, we must begin with some hopefully clarifying remarks about these expressions. These remarks, I must add, are intended only to make reasonably clear how I shall use these expressions; they are not to be taken as an account of Tillich's own usage.

Let us begin with a rather mundane example. Suppose that you look at an electric light and then close your eyes. As G. E. Moore notes, ". . . it sometimes happens that you see, for some little time, against the dark background which you usually see when your eyes are shut, a bright patch similar in shape to the light at which you have just been looking."[16] Of such a bright patch—an example of what some psychologists have called "after images"—we may say that it is *subjective*. By this I mean that it exists only in the mind of the one who experiences it.[17] Thus one sense which we may attach to the word 'subjective' is the following: x is subjective provided that x exists only in the mind of the one who experiences x. Suppose, to shift to

---

[16] G. E. Moore, "Proof of an External World," *Philosophical Papers* (New York: Collier Books, 1962), p. 133.

[17] Suppose someone else performs the same experiment, with similar results. Does he see the *same* bright patch as you? Although there are difficulties that cannot be discussed here, I shall adopt the view, taken by Moore, Ayer, and others, that, although what he sees may be qualitatively the same as what you see, it is, nevertheless, numerically different from the bright patch you see. The difficulties connected with this view do not, I believe, affect the basic distinctions I am endeavoring to make concerning 'subjective' and 'objective'.

another example, that you look at a white wall. The white area or surface of the wall that you see is not subjective in the sense just explained. The white patch of wall that you see does not exist only in your mind, it exists independently of your perception of it. We may say of this white patch of wall that it is *objective*. By this I mean that it exists independently of the mind of the one (or anyone) who experiences it. We may say that whereas the bright patch has only *subjective existence,* the white patch has *objective existence.*

Although the distinction I have made between subjective and objective is quite rough, I think it will suffice for the purpose at hand: namely, to determine whether the phenomenological approach can establish that the holy is objective, rather than simply subjective. Given the meaning I have attached to 'subjective' and 'objective', I think we must conclude that the phenomenological approach cannot establish the objective existence of the holy. For it is precisely this sort of issue that the phenomenological method is designed to avoid. Indeed, I take it that this is Tillich's point in saying, "Phenomenology cannot raise the question of validity of the phenomena it makes visible." Elsewhere he makes similar comments:

It is the aim of the so-called phenomenological method to describe "meanings," disregarding, for the time being, the question of the reality to which they refer.

The test of a phenomenological description is that the picture given by it is convincing, that it can be seen by anyone who is willing to look in the same direction, that the description illuminates other related ideas, and that it makes the reality which these ideas are supposed to reflect understandable. Phenomenology is a way of pointing to phenomena as they "give themselves," without the interference of negative or positive prejudices and explanations (ST, 1:106).

The general point I am making, and which I suggest Tillich is also expressing in the above quotations, is that a phenomenological description of the content of a given experience is *neutral* with respect to the question of whether that content is subjective or objective in the sense explained above. Thus the phenomenological description of the holy has no *logical* implication for the question of whether the holy is subjective or objective. And, if this is so, the phenomenological approach certainly cannot establish that the quality of ultimacy experienced as embodied in the concrete content (religious symbol) of ultimate concern is identical with the ultimate of ontology, being-itself.

The distinction I have drawn between subjective and objective is an ontological, not a phenomenological distinction. It raises a question about the reality of the phenomena of our experience. There is, I believe, another contrast between subjective and objective that is phenomenological in character. And in terms of this contrast the phenomenological approach can, perhaps, establish that the content of an experience is objective, not subjective. Although I find this contrast between subjective and objective extraordinarily difficult to clarify, it is an important distinction and one which is rather fundamental to our investigation of *the holy* and its relation to the ontological ultimate, being-itself. Perhaps this phenomenological contrast between subjective and objective can be gleaned from a consideration of certain remarks made by Rudolf Otto in *The Idea of the Holy*.

In Chapter III of his justly famous work, Otto begins his analysis of the experience of the holy by raising several objections to Schleiermacher's attempt to isolate the essential element in this experience, an element which Schleiermacher called "the feeling of absolute dependence." Otto's first major objection is that in distinguishing the religious feeling of dependence from all other feelings of dependence by calling the former 'absolute' and the latter 'relative', Schleiermacher has made the difference between them only one of degree, rather than a difference of kind. Thus he has failed, according to Otto, to adequately depict the utter *uniqueness* of the experience of the holy. Perhaps Otto would object for a similar reason to Tillich's distinction between an 'ultimate' concern and a 'preliminary' concern. But this objection to Schleiermacher is not of vital importance for our inquiry. It is his second major objection which is of crucial importance here. However, it is because of the first objection that Otto suggests a *name*—rather than Schleiermacher's *descriptive phrase* "the feeling of absolute dependence"—for that element in the experience of the holy which Schleiermacher took to be the *essential* element. His name for that element is "creature-feeling."

Otto's second major objection is that Schleiermacher simply failed to depict the really essential element in the experience of the holy. The consequences of this failure are two. First, Schleiermacher was driven to *subjectivism,* making the essence of religious experience to be an awareness of one's own *self* as absolutely dependent. Second, Schleiermacher was led to regard *God* not as something of which you are *immediately aware* but as something that must be reached as the result of an inference; namely, as the *cause* of one's absolute dependence, which alone is immediately experienced. The paragraph in which Otto makes this objection is extremely important for our purpose and worth quoting in full.

We have now to note a second defect in the formulation of Schleier-macher's principle. The religious category discovered by him, by whose means he professes to determine the real content of the religious emotion, is merely a category of *self*-valuation, in the sense of self-depreciation. According to him the religious emotion would be directly and primarily a sort of *self*-consciousness, a feeling concerning oneself in a special, determined relation, viz. one's dependence. Thus, according to Schleiermacher, I can only come upon the very fact of God as the result of an inference, that is, by reasoning to a cause beyond myself to account for my 'feeling of dependence'. But this is entirely opposed to the psychological facts of the case. Rather, the 'creature-feeling' is itself a first subjective concomitant and effect of another feeling-element, which casts it like a shadow, but which in itself indubitably has immediate and primary reference to an object outside the self.[18]

Otto's objection, simply put, is that Schleiermacher's creature-feeling, far from being the essential feature of the feeling of the numinous, is in fact a subjective, concomitant by-product of the really essential feature—the awareness of the numinous or holy as *objective*, as existing outside of and independent of the self. In short, the essence of religious experience is not consciousness of self as absolutely dependent (Schleiermacher) but consciousness of another as holy (Otto). Indeed, Otto maintains, it is the latter that gives rise to the former, although the former occurs concomitantly with the latter. The essential element in religious experience is not awareness of self but awareness of another—something objective and outside of the self—as holy.

Our problem is to understand what is meant by saying that the numinous is *objective*. Otto might mean that the numinous exists independently of our experience of it. That is, he might mean that the numinous is 'objective' in the ontological sense introduced earlier. But if he means

---

[18] Otto, *The Idea of the Holy*, p. 10.

this I think we can object that he has said nothing in the passage quoted to justify such a claim. For in the passage quoted he seems simply to be stating what, against Schleiermacher, he takes to be the essential element in the experience of the holy. That is, he appears to be giving a phenomenological description of the essential element in the numinous feeling. And, as we have seen, the pure description of the content of the experience is *neutral* so far as the question of whether the content has subjective existence or objective existence is concerned. A phenomenological description of the content of an experience has no ontological implication for that content. What we need here is a sense of 'objective' that is phenomenological, not ontological.

Perhaps another example from perception will be of assistance. It is well known that after-images may be seen not only with eyes closed—our previous example of the bright patch—but also with eyes opened. G. E. Moore reports that he once cut out a four-pointed star from a piece of white paper, placed it on a black background, looked intently at it for some time, and then turned his eyes to a white sheet of paper. He remarks:

. . . and I did find that I saw a grey patch for some little time— I not only saw a grey patch, but I saw it *on* the white ground, and also this grey patch was of roughly the same shape as the white four pointed star at which I had 'looked steadfastly' just before— it also was a four-pointed star. I repeated this simple experiment successfully several times. Now each of those grey four-pointed stars, one of which I saw in each experiment, was what is called an 'after-image' or 'after-sensation'; and can anybody deny that each of these after-images can be quite properly said to have been 'presented in space'? I saw each of them on a real white background, and, if so, each of them was 'presented' on a real white background. But though they were 'presented in space' everybody, I think, would feel that it was gravely misleading to say that they were 'to be met with in space.' The white star at which I 'looked steadfastly,' the black ground on which I saw it, and the white ground on which I saw the after-images, were, of course, 'to be met with in space': they were, in fact, 'physical objects' or surfaces of physical objects. But one important difference between them, on the one hand, and the grey after-images, on the other, can be quite naturally expressed by saying that the latter were *not* 'to be met with in space.'[19]

The phenomenological sense of 'objective' that I am trying to mark off from the ontological sense introduced can, I think, be clarified by using the present example as an analogy. Instead of introducing 'objective' in the sense explained above we might say, in terms of our present example, that x is objective provided that x exists in physical space. In this sense it is clear that the *white* four-pointed start is objective; whereas, the gray four-pointed star, the after-image, is not objective. But we may also give 'objective' a phenomenological sense; namely, x is objective provided that x is *experienced as* being in physical space or, to paraphrase Moore, *presented as* being in physical space. In this phenomenological sense of 'objective' I should say that both the white four-pointed star and the gray four-pointed star are objective. Thus something that is objective in the phenomenological sense may or may not be objective in the ontological sense—existing in physical space. We may, then, for cases of *visual perception* of objects, using 'object' quite broadly to cover after-images as well as physical objects, use 'objective' and 'subjective' in both an ontological and a phenomenological sense.

Ontological:

> x is *subjective* provided that x does not exist in physical space.
>
> x is *objective* provided that x does exist in physical space.

---

19 G. E. Moore, *Philosophical Papers,* pp. 130–31.

Phenomenological:

   x is *subjective* provided that *x* is not experienced as, presented as, being in physical space.

   x is *objective* provided that *x* is experienced as, presented
   as, being in physical space.

The white four-pointed star that Moore saw is objective
in the phenomenological sense and objective in the ontological sense as well. The gray four-pointed star that Moore
saw is objective in the phenomenological sense but *not* objective in the ontological sense; it is subjective in the ontological sense. The bright patch—the after-image seen with
eyes closed—is, I believe, subjective in both the ontological
and the phenomenological sense. For, while we might be
inclined to say that an after-image seen with closed eyes is
presented in *a* space, we cannot say that it is presented in
physical space—when your eyes are shut you are not seeing
any part of physical space at all.

   Having developed the analogy we may now return to
Otto's description of religious experience as an awareness
of a numinous object as objective and outside the self. My
suggestion is that just as it is one thing for an object to be
in physical space and another thing for an object to be presented as in physical space, so, perhaps, it is one thing for
an object or quality to exist outside of and independent of
the self, and quite another thing for an object or quality to
be experienced as, presented as, or felt as existing outside
of and independent of the self. We may, I am suggesting,
experience something as 'out there', as existing independently of us, as 'grasping us'. In thus describing what
we have experienced we are not implying that it *does exist*
independently of us, only that we experience it *as* independent of us, as something 'out there'. The creature-feel-

ing is experienced as 'in here', as something having no existence apart from the self. But the numinous object is not experienced 'in here'. It is, in Otto's own phrase, "*felt as objective and outside the self.*"[20] However, this is consistent, I am maintaining, with the view that the numinous has no existence apart from the self; that is, that the numinous has only subjective existence in the ontological sense.

Although the phenomenological approach may establish (1) that the holy is a quality of ultimacy experienced as embodied in finite objects and (2) that the holy is objective in the phenomenological sense, it cannot establish that this quality of ultimacy is identical with the ultimate of ontology, being-itself, for the simple reason that the phenomenological approach has no implications regarding the ontological status of that which it discovers and describes. I take it that it is this limitation of the phenomenological approach to which Tillich is referring when he remarks, "Phenomenology cannot raise the question of validity of the phenomena it makes visible." The phenomenological description of the holy leaves unanswered the question as to whether the holy is the ontological ultimate or simply a subjective quality that, for whatever psychological reasons, human beings project onto certain objects in their environment. Tillich's view, of course, is that the quality of ultimacy that is experienced as embodied in the concrete content of ultimate concern is not subjective, a projection due to some quirk of human nature, but is, indeed, identical with the philosophical absolute, being-itself. But to establish that this is so, he sees the necessity of supplementing the phenomenological approach with philosophical argument and analysis.

---

[20] Otto, *The Idea of the Holy*, p. 11. (Italics mine.)

In Chapter I, I stated and briefly explained the metaphysical line of reasoning which lies behind Tillich's claim that ultimate concern is directed at being-itself *via* religious symbols. Tillich speaks of this approach as the ontological way of "reaching the referent of religious symbols." Of this approach he remarks:

> It analyzes the kind of being man is, in interdependence with his world. It analyzes the finitude of the finite in different directions, it points to the anxiety which is connected with the awareness of one's finitude, and it raises the question of being-itself, the *prius* of everything that is. The approach tries to find the referent of religious symbolism not in a particular experience, that of the holy and of ultimate concern implied in the holy, but it tries to find it in the character of being as such, in everything that is.[21]

My purpose here is not primarily to explain and evaluate Tillich's ontological system but to exhibit the role that it plays in his account of the phenomena of religious experience. Its primary role, as I see it, is one of explanation. One possible explanation of the phenomenological facts of religious experience—that is, of the Tillich-Otto account of those facts—is the Freudian theory, a view that interprets the holy as a projection due to unconscious impulses arising out of the experiences of early childhood, etc.[22] Tillich accepts certain aspects of the Freudian projection theory so far as the gods of various religions are concerned. But the holy, the numinous quality, is not, he thinks, best explained as a projection. Given his ontology, Tillich thinks, and perhaps rightly, that the most reasonable explanation of the quality of ultimacy is one which identifies it with the ultimate of ontology, being-itself. The gods, as beings

---

[21] Tillich, "The Meaning and Justification of Religious Symbols," *Religious Experience and Truth*, p. 7.

[22] See "The Religious Symbol," *Religious Experience and Truth*, pp. 305–6, for some detailed criticisms of Freud by Tillich.

who are supra-human in knowledge and power, etc., may be, in part, projections arising from the childhood longing for the father, but the quality of ultimacy which is experienced as embodied in the gods is not itself a projection. The ultimate encountered in religious experience is, on Tillich's account, the ultimate of ontology. Thus he remarks:

> They (the gods) are images of human nature or subhuman powers raised to a superhuman realm. This fact, which theologians must face in all its implications, is the basis of all theories of "projection" which say that the gods are simply imaginary projections of elements of finitude, natural and human elements. What these theories disregard is that projection always is projection *on* something—a wall, a screen, another being, another realm. Obviously, it is absurd to class that on which the projection is realized with the projection itself. A screen is not projected; it receives the projection. The realm against which the divine images are projected is not itself a projection. It is the experienced ultimacy of being and meaning. It is the realm of ultimate concern (ST, 1:212).

Tillich frequently speaks as though there could be no doubt that the phenomenological ultimate of religious experience is identical with the ontological ultimate, being-itself.

> The immediate awareness of the Unconditioned has not the character of faith but of self-evidence (TC, 27).

> Faith is certain in so far as it is an experience of the holy (DF, 16).

> Only certain is the ultimacy as ultimacy, the infinite passion as infinite passion (DF, 17).

How are we to understand these remarks? There are, it seems to me, three possible interpretations that can be given of Tillich's claim that in religious experience one may be absolutely certain that one has encountered the ultimate. First, Tillich may mean simply that when you are ultimately concerned about something x you are, or at least may be, certain that your attitude toward x is one of ultimate concern. Second, Tillich may mean that you may be certain that you have experienced x as embodying the quality of ultimacy. As Tillich acknowledges, the term 'ultimate concern' is meant to refer both to the ultimacy of your concern about x and to the ultimacy that you experience as embodied in x.

> The term 'ultimate concern' unites the subjective and the objective side of the act of faith—the *fides qua creditur* (the faith through which one believes) and the *fides quae creditur* (the faith which is believed). The first is the classical term for the centered act of the personality, the ultimate concern. The second is the classical term for that toward which this act is directed, the ultimate itself, expressed in symbols of the divine. This distinction is important, but not ultimately so, for the one side cannot be without the other (DF, 10).

Between these two possibilities it is clear, I think, that the second is the one about which Tillich is claiming we may be certain. (This is not to imply that he thinks we cannot be certain about the first.) Thus I take him to be claiming that one may be absolutely certain that he has experienced the quality of ultimacy as embodied in the concrete content of ultimate concern. The third possibility arises out of the second. Tillich may mean that one may be absolutely certain that he has experienced the ontological ultimate as embodied in the concrete content. It will facilitate matters if the second and third interpretations are set forth and the difference between them discussed:

2. One may be absolutely certain that he has experienced the quality of ultimacy.
3. One may be absolutely certain that in experiencing the quality of ultimacy he has experienced the ontological ultimate.

The difference between 2 and 3 is that 2 leaves open the question concerning the ontological status of the ultimacy one is certain he has experienced. Point 3 makes the ontological status of the quality of ultimacy a matter of immediate certainty. Item 2, of course, does not imply that the quality of ultimacy is *not* the ontological ultimate; it simply refrains from including this as part of what is given as absolutely certain. As I have indicated, Tillich is claiming 2, but he may be claiming 3 as well. That is, he may be claiming that we are certain not only that we have encountered ultimacy, but also that the ultimacy is the ontological ultimate.

The issue before us is a subtle one. There is no question but that Tillich holds (A) that the ultimacy encountered in the concrete content (religious symbol) *is* the ontological ultimate. There is no question but that Tillich holds that in the state of ultimate concern one is absolutely certain that he has experienced the quality of ultimacy. The question is: Does he also hold that in the state of ultimate concern one is absolutely certain that the quality of ultimacy is the ontological ultimate? That is, although he clearly holds 2, does he hold 3 as well? I am inclined to think that he does. But we must proceed with caution here. It is important to note that A and 2 do not *justify* Tillich in holding 3—if, indeed, he does hold 3. For we must observe that 'certainty' is an *intensional* term. Hence, it does not follow from (a) Jones is certain that he has experienced x, and (b) x is identical with y, that (c) Jones is certain that he has experienced y. For example, Jones may be certain that he saw Smith, Smith may be identical with the murderer of Brown, and yet Jones may not be certain that he saw the murderer of Brown. Similarly, 3 does not follow from *A* and 2.

What leads me to suggest that perhaps Tillich holds 3, as well as 2, is that when he discusses the element of certainty and the element of risk that are included in every act of faith he never mentions the possibility that the quality of ultimacy may not be the ontological ultimate as included in the element of risk. The element of risk has to do *solely* with the way in which the concrete content is related to the quality of ultimacy, never with the quality of ultimacy as such.

Faith contains a contingent element and demands a risk. It combines the ontological certainty of the Unconditioned with the uncertainty about everything conditioned and concrete. . . . The risk of faith is based on the fact that the unconditional element can become a matter of ultimate concern only if it appears in a concrete embodiment (TC, 27–28).

The risk of faith is not arbitrariness; it is a unity of fate and decision. And it is based on a foundation which is not risk: the awareness of the unconditional element in ourselves and our world (TC, 28).

But, as we shall see in the last chapter, getting clear on these passages and other remarks Tillich makes about the risk of idolatry is no easy task. Hence, it is with considerable hesitation that I make the suggestion that Tillich's view is that the one who is ultimately concerned is *certain* that in experiencing the quality of the holy he has experienced what is ontologically ultimate. Perhaps, then, it is best here simply to indicate what, in my own view, Tillich is *entitled* to say on this matter—leaving aside the question of what he actually says.

In terms of his ontological analysis of man and his world Tillich is led to the conclusion that 'being-itself' designates what is ontologically ultimate and that man has an immediate *awareness* of the ontological ultimate. "Man . . . is aware of the Unconditioned" (TC, 24). "It is obvious that the ontological awareness is immediate, and not mediated by inferential processes. It is present, whenever conscious attention is focussed on it, in terms of an unconditional certainty" (TC, 23). Given this ontological conclusion and the phenomenological description of ultimate concern as an awareness of the quality of ultimacy embodied in some finite object, Tillich is entitled to conclude, it seems to me, that the holy encountered in ultimate concern *is* the ontological ultimate, being-itself. But even here I should think that Tillich should allow that one might have an experience which—so far as that *particular* experience is concerned—is phenomenologically indistinguishable from the awareness of the ontological ultimate, and yet be a delusory experience in the sense of an experience of a quality that has no reality apart from the self who experiences it. So far as I can determine, he never considers this possibility. There is, for Tillich, no distinction to be drawn between a veridical and a delusory experience of ultimacy. Every experience of what is phenomenologically ultimate is an experience of what is ontologically ultimate. However, ignoring this difficulty, we may conclude that, given his premises, Tillich is entitled to maintain that the ultimate of religious experience is the ultimate of ontology.

It is, however, one thing for Tillich to be certain that the religious man who experiences the holy, experiences what is ontologically ultimate, and quite another thing for the religious man to be certain. For, as I have presented it, the certainty that in experiencing the holy one has experienced what is ontologically ultimate is not given with the experience of the holy but results from an ontological *inter-pretation* of that experience. I conclude, therefore, that Tillich is not entitled to claim, without qualification, that one may be absolutely certain that in experiencing the quality of ultimacy he has experienced the ontological ultimate. The qualification is that this certainty can be attained, if at all, only if the individual arrives at the ontological conclusion stated above and interprets his experience in accordance with that conclusion.

Before discussing the different kinds of religious symbols and their combination into myths, a summary of the main points that have emerged thus far may be useful. I began this chapter by suggesting that Tillich endeavors to distinguish religious symbols from non-religious symbols by holding that religious symbols alone point to being-itself and are the foci of ultimate concern. Certain difficulties in the claim that religious symbols point to (signify) being-itself were discussed, and it was argued that the relationship of signification in which these symbols stand to being-itself is not the result of conscious decision but must be conceived as due wholly to unconscious needs and processes. I then argued that although it may be true that religious symbols point to being-itself, this truth would not provide us with an effective means of discriminating between religious and non-religious symbols. Being the foci of ultimate concern was, I suggested, the actual criterion by which Tillich determines the members of the class of religious symbols. The claim that being-itself is the referent of religious symbols was, I argued, intended as an explanation for the fact that men direct ultimate concern at finite objects (religious symbols). The central question that then emerged was: How does Tillich endeavor to establish that being-itself, the metaphysical ultimate, is the referent of religious symbolism? In answering this question we first noted that Tillich is careful to distinguish two approaches —the phenomenological and the ontological—in the problem of determining the referent of religious symbols. The phenomenological approach apparently can establish that in the experience of ultimate concern the concrete content is transformed and transcended; it embodies a unique, indescribable quality of ultimacy, the holy. Can the phenomenological approach establish that the holy, this quality of ultimacy, is the ontological ultimate, being-itself? I argued that although the pure description of religious experience can establish that the holy is phenomenologically objective, it cannot establish that the holy is the ontological ultimate. Moreover, it was suggested that Tillich acknowledges this limitation of the phenomenological approach. The ontological approach, I suggested, is to be viewed as one of several possible explanations of the phenomenologically established facts of religious experience. On the basis of ontological analysis and argument Tillich endeavors to establish that man has an immediate awareness of what is ontologically ultimate, being-itself. Thus armed, he examines religious experience and concludes that the quality of ultimacy experienced as embodied in religious symbols is being-itself. Finally, I examined Tillich's claim that one may be absolutely certain that he has experienced the ultimate and argued that only on the basis of a particular ontological interpretation of what is given in religious experience would one be justified in holding that in experiencing the ultimate one may be certain that he has experienced what is ontologically ultimate.

❧VI❧

Religious Symbols and Myths

HAVING discussed Tillich's view of the essential nature of a religious symbol, we must now examine in some detail his classification of religious symbols into different levels and groups, and his account of religious myths.

In his writings on symbolism Tillich has endeavored to distinguish various 'types' or 'levels' of religious symbols. There appear to be two basic distinctions he is anxious to make. One distinction is between two *levels* of religious symbols, a 'transcendent level' and an 'immanent level.' "There are two fundamental levels in all religious symbols: the transcendent level, the level which goes *beyond* the empirical reality we encounter, and the immanent level, the level which we find *within* the encounter with reality" (TC, 61). A second distinction is between two *kinds* of religious symbols, 'primary' and 'secondary.'[1] If I understand Tillich, primary religious symbols are those which 'represent' the ultimate, being-itself; whereas secondary

---

[1] Tillich, "The Meaning and Justification of Religious Symbols," *Religious Experience and Truth*, ed. Sidney Hook (New York: New York University Press, 1961), p. 8.

religious symbols are those which 'support' and/or 'symbolize' symbols on the primary level. Of secondary religious symbols Tillich has little to say. Therefore, I shall not undertake an account of them. It is clear that his main concern is to describe those religious symbols he calls 'primary.' Our first concern must be to relate these two basic sets of distinctions.

When Tillich's discussion of primary religious symbols is carefully compared with his discussion of transcendent level and immanent level symbols, it becomes clear that the distinction between two levels of religious symbolism is a distinction *within* primary religious symbols. Thus, within the class of primary religious symbols—that is, symbols which "point directly to the referent of all religious symbolism"—we are to distinguish two basic sub-classes; namely, a class of transcendent level symbols and a class of immanent level symbols. Primary religious symbols on the transcendent level all concern *God*. Here Tillich distinguishes (*a*) God himself as a symbol, (*b*) the qualities and attributes of God as symbols, and (*c*) the actions of God as symbols. Primary religious symbols on the immanent level concern the appearances of the divine in the realm of empirical reality. "Here we have first of all the incarnations of the divine, . . . divine beings transmuted into animals or men or any kinds of other beings as they appear in time and space" (TC, 63).

Tillich's view that God himself is a symbol is quite difficult to understand. For he seems to hold that the religious idea of God is only *partly* symbolic. Thus he remarks:

But we cannot simply say that God is a symbol. We must always say two things about him: we must say that there is a non-symbolic element in our image of God—namely, that he is ultimate reality, being-itself, ground of being, power of being; and the other, that he is the highest being in which everything that we have does exist in the most perfect way. If we say this we have in our mind the image of a highest being, a being with the characteristics of highest perfection. That means we have a symbol for that which is not symbolic in the idea of God—namely, "Being Itself" (TC, 61).

One difficulty this passage raises is how we can render it consistent with Tillich's view, discussed in Chapter I, that God is being-itself and with the view of the ordinary religious man that God is the supremely perfect being. That is, the passage quoted seems to imply that 'God' means both a supremely perfect being and being-itself. Tillich's own view, discussed earlier, seems to be that 'God' means being-itself, and the plain religious man is likely to mean by 'God' no more or less than the supremely perfect being.

The solution to this difficulty is, I think, as follows: Tillich does wish to identify God with being-itself, to use the term 'God' to designate solely the unconditionally transcendent. But we are not to construe his view that 'God' means being-itself as a report about the use of the word 'God' in a religious setting, as a report of the meaning ordinarily attached to the word 'God'. Rather, I think we must construe Tillich's "definition" of 'God' as a proposal, the justification for which is its usefulness in solving theoretical problems. Thus, just as the physicist may use ordinary terms—'matter', 'energy', etc.,—in technical ways for theoretical purposes, so the philosophical-theologian may take terms from ordinary religious discourse and give them a technical sense for theoretical purposes. However, it would be a mistake to represent Tillich as introducing a technical meaning for the term 'God' which in *his* view has no connection with the more familiar notion of God. For, if I understand Tillich, his view is that in the ordinary religious man's conception of God the idea of being-itself is already contained. Thus, even though the plain religious man may have no concept of being-itself, Tillich is, I think, maintaining that as a matter of fact being-itself is an element in his idea of God. This is highly paradoxical and needs explanation.

It should be clear by now that on Tillich's theory—involving as it does both a phenomenological description of religious experience and an ontological interpretation of that experience—what is essential and common to religious experience is the encounter with the holy, with being-itself. Since the holy is felt as ultimate and transcendent, and since in trying to conceive of the holy the religious man is bound by his finitude to concrete imagery, he inevitably is led to conceive of the holy as the highest possible *object*, in short, as the supremely perfect being. This, in brief, is Tillich's explanation for the emergence of the conception of God as the supreme being. The important point, however, is that the idea of a supremely perfect being is the religious man's way of representing what transcends the realm of the concrete altogether, being-itself.

The divine beings and the Supreme Being, God, are representations of that which is ultimately referred to in the religious act. They are representations, for the unconditioned transcendent surpasses every possible conception of a being, including even the conception of a Supreme Being.[2]

We have, then, the following situation. The religious man may quite naturally mean by 'God' the supremely perfect being. But since, on Tillich's view, the notion of a

[2] Tillich, "The Religious Symbol," *Religious Experience and Truth,* p. 314.

supremely perfect being is the result of the religious man's effort—however unconscious it may be—to form an appropriate religious conception of what is experienced—being-itself—Tillich concludes that the religious man's conception of God has a double meaning, as it were. On the one hand it certainly means a transcendent object, the supremely perfect being. But, on the other hand, it also means the absolutely transcendent, being-itself.

> But the word "God" involves a double meaning: it connotes the unconditioned transcendent, the ultimate, and also an object somehow endowed with qualities and actions. The first is not figurative or symbolic, but is rather in the strictest sense what it is said to be. The second, however, is really symbolic, figurative. It is the second that is the object envisaged by the religious consciousness. The idea of a Supreme Being possessing certain definite qualities is present in the consciousness. But the religious consciousness is also aware of the fact that when the word "God" is heard, this idea is figurative, that it does not signify an object, that is, it must be transcendent. The word "God" produces a contradiction in the consciousness, it involves something figurative that we really have in mind and that is represented by this idea. In the word "God" is contained at the same time that which actually functions as a representation and also the idea that it is *only* a representation. It has the peculiarity of transcending its own conceptual content—upon this depends the numinous character that the word has in science and in life in spite of every misuse through false objectification. God as an object is a representation of the reality ultimately referred to in the religious act, but in the word "God" this objectivity is negated and at the same time its representative character is asserted.[3]

Tillich may be involved in a semantic confusion in holding that the word 'God' has this double meaning. He may also be mistaken on a matter of fact in claiming that the religious consciousness is *aware* that the word 'God' does not simply signify the highest being. Be that as it may, the principle behind his claim that 'God' has a double mean-

---

[3] *Ibid.*, p. 315.

ing seems to be that since the concept of the supremely perfect being is itself intended as a representation of that which is beyond any concrete conception, we may say that the word 'God' means not only the highest being but also what the concept of the highest being is intended to represent, namely, the holy or being-itself. The *material* point underlying Tillich's semantic remark about the word 'God' as it is used in religious discourse is that the idea or image of the highest being is the religious man's way of *representing* or *portraying* what is not *a* being at all, but what transcends the realm of objects, namely the holy or being-itself.

His view, then, seems to be that the *religious idea of God* designates not only an *object*, the highest being, but also being-itself. His own view of God as being-itself—which we may call the *philosophical idea of God*—amounts to the religious idea of God *minus* its concrete, symbolic element. From his point of view this is a refinement on the religious idea since it separates out the symbolic content and focuses on what he regards as the essential, common element in the religious encounter. If we ask why the religious conception of God contains the symbolic notion of a highest being, why it does not contain simply the nonsymbolic notion of being-itself, Tillich's answer, presumably, would be that the religious man endeavors to conceive of the ultimate as it is encountered in the religious life. Since it is impossible for man to encounter the ultimate apart from some concrete content, the closest he can come to the ultimate is in terms of that content which most closely approximates the true ultimate, namely, the image of a transcendent being embodying the highest qualities known to man, carried to their highest degree.

If we adopt Tillich's proposal and simply identify God with the nonsymbolic element in what he takes to be the religious idea of God, I think we can then understand Tillich's view about religious symbols—both linguistic and non-linguistic—and how that view differs from more traditional accounts of religious symbolism. Non-linguistic religious symbols result from the fact that the nonsymbolic element can be encountered only in something concrete. Thus something concrete—a person, a statue, a goal—becomes the focus of ultimate concern and 'represents' the ultimate object of concern—God, being-itself. Linguistic religious symbols arise from the need to talk about God and from the fact that being-itself, God, cannot be described, or otherwise talked about, in nonsymbolic language. The reason God, being-itself, cannot be talked about in literal terms is, as we saw in Chapter I, that language is subject to what Tillich calls "the structure of being" and can be applied literally only to entities that are subject to that structure. Since being-itself is not subject to the structure of being, it cannot be spoken about literally, but only symbolically. This seems to be the main point of the following passage:

As we already have seen, God as being-itself is the ground of the ontological structure of being without being subject to this structure himself. . . . Therefore, if anything beyond this bare assertion is said about God, it no longer is a direct and proper statement, no longer a concept. It is indirect, and it points to something beyond itself. In a word, it is symbolic (ST, 1:239).

We can put Tillich's point in another way. His view is that the primary meaning of a predicate expression is inextricable from the *use* of that expression to talk about, describe, etc., beings—that is, entities subject to the structure of being. The literal or primary meaning of a predicate expression implies or presupposes that the expression is used to talk about entities subject to the structure of being. A predicate expression therefore cannot be applied literally beyond the structure of being. When a predicate expression is applied beyond the structure of being, as when we talk of God, being-itself, it must be used as a metaphor or a symbol; otherwise we produce either nonsense or contradiction. "Man's ultimate concern must be expressed symbolically, because symbolic language alone is able to express the ultimate" (DF, 41).

The radical nature of Tillich's theory of religious myths and symbols—or, more generally, religious discourse about God—is a logical consequence of (1) his view that God is not *a* being, even a highest being, and (2) his claim that predicate expressions are logically tied (by virtue of their primary meaning) to beings. The radical nature of his theory can be exhibited by contrasting it with a more traditional theory of religious discourse about God. Traditionally, theologians and thoughtful religious men have regarded God as an infinite, immaterial, omnipotent, omniscient, perfectly good *being*. Accordingly, they have distinguished between predicate expressions which in their primary meaning refer either to parts of a body (e.g., 'hand', 'face') or to activities impossible without a body (e.g. 'walking', 'drinking') and predicate expressions which in their primary meaning refer to properties of a mind or mental activities (e.g., 'wise', 'good', 'merciful', 'loving'). Expressions of the first kind cannot be predicated *properly* (i.e., with their primary meaning) of God. For, since God does not have a body, to apply them properly to him would result either in contradiction or nonsense. Thus, such expressions may be predicated of God only metaphorically or symbolically. Expressions of the second kind, it is argued, can be predicated *properly* of God; however, it is generally pointed out that the properties designated by 'good', 'wisdom', etc., occur in God in the highest possible degree—thus God is said to be infinitely good, infinitely wise, etc.

Some philosophers have criticized the traditional view by claiming that the *criteria* for applying expressions of the second sort involve physical behavior. Since God has no body, it is argued that we have no criteria for applying these expressions (in their primary meaning) to him. Other philosophers have claimed that expressions of the second kind ('good', 'merciful', etc.) involve, as part of their *meaning,* a reference to bodily behavior. Thus one philosopher recently said that when predicated of God ". . . all these words lose their meaning if we are told that God does not possess a body. . . . For what would it be like to be, say, just, without a body? To be just a person has to *act* justly—he has to behave in certain ways. This is not reductive materialism. It is a simple empirical truth about what we mean by 'just'. But how is it possible to perform these acts, to behave in the required ways without a body?"[4] Tillich's rejection of the traditional view, however, does not depend on claiming that expressions of the second sort are logically tied—either by way of their criteria for application or their primary meaning—to bodily behavior. His rejection depends simply on the claim that expressions of the second kind, as well as of the first, can be *properly* predicated only of *beings.* Since this is so, it is

---

4 Paul Edwards, "Some Notes on Anthropomorphic Theology," *Religious Experience and Truth,* p. 243.

clear that the statement "God (being-itself) is merciful" becomes contradictory or nonsense if "merciful" is used in its primary sense. If it is objected that the ordinary religious man means to be talking about a supreme being and not being-itself when he says "God is merciful," Tillich, perhaps, would agree. But he would then argue, as we have seen, that this traditional conception of God is itself a *symbol* for *God* as being-itself. This is the meaning of his cryptic remark "God is the symbol of God" (DF, 46). That is, God (conceived as the supreme being) is a symbol for God (conceived as being-itself).

Having discussed Tillich's view of (*a*) God himself as a symbol, we may now give some account of (*b*) the qualities and attributes of God as symbols, and (*c*) the actions of God as symbols. Perhaps the first point that needs noting is that Tillich here seems to be discussing *linguistic* religious symbols. That is, he is trying to explain the symbolic character of what I have called theological or religious statements—statements whose subject term is 'God'. These statements are of two sorts, according to whether they ascribe *qualities* or *activities* to God. A few examples will facilitate our discussion.

1. God is omnipotent.
2. God is living.
3. God is just.
4. God created the world.
5. God has sent His son.

Examples 1 to 3 ascribe certain qualities or attributes to God. Examples 4 and 5 ascribe certain actions to God. Our task here is to explicate and evaluate Tillich's account of the symbolic character of these statements.

In Chapter I we saw that Tillich's strategy is to translate theological statements about God into ontological statements about being-itself. From the foregoing discussion of God himself as a symbol, it should be clear that on Tillich's view such a translation is not only justified by his philosophical idea of God as being-itself, but also justified by the religious idea of God. For we saw that on his view the religious idea of God contains both a symbolic and a nonsymbolic element. The concept of a supremely perfect being represents the nonsymbolic element, being-itself. The idea of a supreme being is *symbolic* because (*a*) it is the religious man's way of representing being-itself and (*b*) being-itself—as we have seen—cannot be conceived or talked about in other than symbolic language. It would seem, then, that on Tillich's theory, statements 1 through 5 are symbolic solely by virtue of his claim that their subject term 'God' represents or stands for being-itself. It is because 'God' is taken to stand for being-itself—explicitly by Tillich and implicitly, he maintains, by plain religious men —that statements 1 through 5 are symbolic statements.

It is important to distinguish between explaining *why* 1 through 5 are symbolic statements on Tillich's theory, and explaining *what,* on his theory, the symbolic statements may be understood to express. The explanation of why 1 through 5 are symbolic is, I think, quite clear. They are symbolic because on Tillich's view they are about being-itself and, as was argued in Chapter I, no literal, positive statement can be made about being-itself. But it is one thing to explain why statements 1 through 5 must be understood to have a symbolic rather than a literal meaning, and it is quite another thing to explain, for each of these statements, *what* its symbolic meaning is. The really fundamental, perhaps insoluble, problems in Tillich's account of linguistic religious symbols arise when we ask what is *meant* by a religious statement on his theory. Indeed, it is Tillich's explanation of *why* religious statements are symbolic—namely, that they are about being-itself—that creates the problems which arise in explaining what is meant by particular religious statements.

In Chapter I, I suggested that there is something wrong with Tillich's proposed elucidation of our admittedly symbolic discourse about God in terms of ontological statements about being-itself. There seems to be something wrong because on his own view being-itself is ineffable and, consequently, statements about being-itself must also be symbolic. But if this is so then the ontological statements about being-itself seem as much in need of elucidation as the ideological statements about God they were to elucidate. In short, if to interpret or explain what is meant by a symbolic or metaphorical statement S is to produce another statement S' which expresses in *nonsymbolic* terms essentially what S expresses in *symbolic* terms, it is *impossible* on Tillich's theory to ever explain or interpret *any* religious statement about God. For, since 'God' stands for being-itself, the symbolic statement about God would be correctly interpreted only by some ontological statement about being-itself. But, since 'being-itself' is ineffable, every ontological statement about being-itself is necessarily symbolic.

The difficulty we have uncovered is, I think, the fundamental problem in Tillich's theory of religious symbolism. It is the source, so far as I can see, of most of the major objections that critics have advanced against his theory. It is necessary, therefore, to examine this problem in some detail.

Perhaps we should begin by noting that Tillich does offer interpretations of religious statements about God in terms of ontological statements about being-itself. Indeed, he thinks it is the business of theology to do so. "Theology should not weaken the concrete symbols, but it must analyze them and interpret them in abstract ontological terms" (ST, 1:242). Two examples of his efforts in this direction are as follows:

In popular parlance the concept "omnipotence" implies a highest being who is able to do whatever he wants. This notion must be rejected, religiously as well as theologically. . . . It is more adequate to define omnipotence as the power of being which resists nonbeing in all its expressions and which is manifest in the creative process in all its forms (ST, 1:273).

Life is the actuality of being, or, more exactly, it is the process in which potential being becomes actual being. But in God as God there is no distinction between potentiality and actuality. Therefore, we cannot speak of God as living in the proper or nonsymbolic sense of the word life. We must speak of God as living in symbolic terms. . . . God lives in so far as he is the ground of life (ST, 1:242).

Concerning these and other interpretations Tillich's critics take the view that he *intends* to be offering *nonsymbolic* translations of religious statements. For example, Alston remarks: "I do not know how to read this other than as an attempt to translate symbolic language into nonsymbolic language."[5] Another critic, Edwards, argues:

Tillich, the dogmatist, does not hesitate to offer translations or what I have called reductions of his "symbolic" statements about God. We can also express literally, for example, what we mean "sym-

---

[5] Alston, *Religious Experience and Truth*, p. 25.

bolically" when we say that God is living. "God lives," the reduction runs, "insofar as he is the ground of life."[6]

> . . . although Tillich gives the impression that the metaphors have
> been eliminated in these and similar cases, this is not so. He
> never seems to have noticed that even in his basic statement,
> when elaborated in terms of "ground" and "structure", these
> words are used metaphorically and not literally.[7]

Against these criticisms, especially Edward's, several
points need to be made.

It must be noted that Tillich nowhere says that the interpretation or translation is itself literal. Indeed, to hold such
a view would be inconsistent with his explicit claim that
every statement about being-itself is symbolic or metaphorical. It is not Tillich but Edwards who gives the 'impression' that Tillich's view is that the translation elimi-
nates the metaphor in the religious statement 'God is living'. It is true, I think, that Tillich would regard the statement (a) 'being-itself is the ground of life' as an essential
part of the interpretation of the religious statement (b)
'God is living'. What is not true is that he regards a as a
translation of b such that a expresses in *literal* terms what
b expresses symbolically.

Having misrepresented Tillich as holding that 'God (being-itself) is the ground of life' is a literal statement, Edwards then correctly points out that 'ground' is being used
metaphorically and not literally. As I have presented matters, this is what should be expected. On Tillich's own
theory, no statement about being-itself can be nonsymbolic. Hence, on Tillich's theory, it is to be expected that

---

6 Paul Edwards, "Professor Tillich's Confusions," *Mind*, 74 (April,
1965): 203–4.

7 *Ibid.*, p. 204.

the interpretation of the religious statement 'God is living' will itself involve a symbolic statement about being-itself. Edward's claim that Tillich "never seems to have noticed" that in the interpretation 'ground' is being used metaphorically is, I am afraid, simply mistaken. Tillich remarks in his "Reply to Interpretation and Criticism": ". . . I agree that 'ground' and 'power' of being are symbolic notions, in so far as they use elements of being (power, cause) in order to circumscribe being-itself."[8]

Alston, unlike Edwards, is careful to acknowledge that Tillich might intend the ontological interpretations of theological statements to be themselves symbolic. Thus, after quoting Tillich's interpretation of theological statements ascribing 'will' and 'intellect' to God as "symbols for dynamics in all its ramifications and for form as the meaningful structure of being-itself," Alston remarks concerning these ontological interpretations:

If they were intended to be simply the replacement of one symbol by another symbol, they would be grotesque failures. No one would suppose that "dynamics in all its ramifications" is a better religious symbol, i.e., performs a symbolic function better or more clearly than "will."[9]

What I have been arguing is that Tillich's ontological interpretations of religious statements are, *on his own theory,* symbolic statements. Admitting that point, we must now see what can be said concerning Alston's criticism. First, it must be admitted that "dynamics in all its ramifications" is not a better *religious* symbol than "will". It is not a better

---

[8] Charles W. Kegley and Robert W. Bretall, eds., *The Theology of Paul Tillich* (New York: Macmillan, 1959), p. 335. Also see ST, 1: 156.

[9] Alston, *Religious Experience and Truth,* p. 25.

religious symbol because it is not a *religious* symbol at all. To speak about being-itself in terms of "dynamics in all its ramifications" is to make an *ontological* statement, not a *religious* statement. To add that "dynamics" is being used metaphorically or symbolically is not to imply that the ontological statement is a religious statement. However, Alston goes on to add that no one would suppose that "dynamics in all its ramifications" "performs a symbolic function better or more clearly than 'will'." Certainly this is true of most religious men; indeed it may be true of all those without some training in metaphysics. But I think we have to ask the question, "better for what purpose?" If the purpose is to marshal religious feelings and actions, to provide concrete images to function as foci for ultimate concern, then there is no question but that "will" is a better symbol than "dynamics in all its ramifications". It would be absurd to think otherwise. However, if the purpose is to understand reality, to get a conceptual grasp, a more accurate picture, of the reality lying behind the concrete imagery of religious symbolism, then perhaps "dynamics in all its ramifications" is a better symbol than "will". Tillich, of course, is not suggesting that the symbolic concepts of his ontology are better *for religious purposes* than the symbolic expressions of religious discourse. He is, I am suggesting, maintaining that they are better if our purpose is to describe the nature of ultimate reality. If Alston intends to claim that they are inferior even for this latter purpose, he needs to support his claim by arguments.

These remarks in defense of Tillich leave untouched, however, what I have argued is the central problem in Tillich's account of linguistic religious symbols. On his theory it seems impossible to break out of the web of symbols. A religious statement S about God is interpreted by Tillich in terms of an ontological statement S' about being-itself. But, since no nonsymbolic positive statement about being-itself is possible on Tillich's theory, S' must also be symbolic. Now, if to interpret or explain what is meant by a symbolic or metaphorical statement S is to produce another statement S' which expresses in *nonsymbolic* terms essentially what S expresses in *symbolic* terms, it follows that it is impossible on Tillich's theory to ever explain or interpret *any* religious statement about God. This conclusion, of course, is disastrous to Tillich's entire theory of religious symbols. We must now see what can be done to avoid it.

There are, I believe, only two things that can be done. One is to abandon the view that being-itself can be described only in symbolic terms. However, since this would result in far reaching changes in Tillich's ontology, as well as in his account of religious symbols, I shall not pursue this possibility. The second is to simply deny the semantic principle that led to the disastrous conclusion. Apart from denying this principle, I see no way in which Tillich's theory can remain intact and avoid the conclusion that it is impossible to interpret or understand any religious statement about God. It is this second possibility that I shall now explore.

What I have called the semantic principle may take various forms. One quite strong form of it is as follows: A symbolic, or metaphorical, statement S is meaningful only if what it expresses can be expressed by some nonsymbolic statement S'. As it stands, however, this principle is quite likely false. For it is very doubtful that a literal statement is *completely* synonymous with the metaphorical statement it translates. What, for example, would be the literal statement which expresses exactly what is expressed by e. e. cummings' metaphorical line, "the sweet small clumsy feet of april came into the ragged meadows of my soul"?[10] Metaphorical statements frequently express nuances of feeling, etc., that their literal interpretations fail to express. Hence, if our principle is not to be obviously false, some restriction must be placed on what the literal statement is expected to express in common with the symbolic statement it purports to translate.

Perhaps it will suffice if we understand the principle to require only that the *cognitive* claims made by the metaphorical statement must be expressible by some nonsymbolic statement, or set of such statements. The symbolic statement, for example, "John is a lion" may express more than the literal statement "John is brave," but it can be argued that the latter suffices to express the cognitive import of the former. Thus we may understand the principle to assert that a symbolic statement which purports to make cognitive claims is meaningful only if those cognitive claims can be made by some nonsymbolic statement. If we understand the principle in this fashion, it is clear, I think, that Tillich's theory of religious symbols is inconsistent with it. That this is so can be most easily shown in terms of an example. Earlier, we noted that 'being-itself is the ground of life' is an ontological statement and is, for Tillich, an essential part, at least, of the correct interpretation of the symbolic, religious statement 'God is living.' Now Tillich is committed to the view that the ontological statement 'being-itself is the ground of life' (a) is symbolic and

---

10 Quoted in William P. Alston, *Philosophy of Language* (Englewood Cliffs, N.J.: Prentice-Hall, 1964), p. 96.

(*b*) possesses cognitive content. But, given our principle, it would follow that this ontological statement is meaningful only if the cognitive content it purports to express can be expressed by some nonsymbolic statement. But to express precisely that cognitive content the *nonsymbolic* statement would surely have to be a statement about being-itself. The latter sort of statement—i.e., a nonsymbolic statement about being-itself—is not, however, possible for Tillich. Hence, given our principle it will follow that the ontological statements about being-itself, and the religious statements about God they purport to interpret, are meaningless. But such a conclusion is surely inconsistent with Tillich's view of religious statements about God and ontological statements about being-itself.

I have been arguing thus far that Tillich's theory of linguistic, religious symbolism is inconsistent with the semantic principle that a symbolic or metaphorical statement is meaningful only if its cognitive content is expressible by some literal statement. If we like we may call those symbolic statements whose cognitive content can be expressed by literal statements "reducible symbolic statements"; those symbolic statements whose purported cognitive content *cannot* be expressed by literal statements we may call "irreducible symbolic statements." Tillich's theory, as I have presented it, implies that there are meaningful, irreducible symbolic statements. Our principle implies that irreducible symbolic statements are *not* meaningful. If our principle is correct, Tillich's theory is incorrect. If Tillich's theory is correct, our principle is incorrect. A third possibility, of course, is that both the principle and the theory are incorrect.

The correctness or incorrectness of the semantic principle we have been discussing is an issue that cannot be settled here, involving, as it does, complicated and controversial issues in the philosophy of language. However, some general remarks concerning its employment against Tillich's theory may be helpful.

It is evident that a principle of the sort we have been considering is made much of in discussions of religious symbolism. For example, in his admirable book on mysticism, W. T. Stace, in the course of objecting to what he calls "the metaphorical theory" of the mystic's descriptions of mystical experiences, uses—without so much as an argument in its behalf—a rough version of our principle which he expresses as, "metaphorical language is only meaningful and justifiable if it is at least theoretically translatable into literal language; . . ."[11] And Edwards, in the course of criticizing Tillich, holds that a metaphorical statement is intelligible only if "the truth-claims made by the sentence in which it occurs can be reproduced by one or more sentences all of whose components are used in literal senses."[12] 'Truth-claims' and 'cognitive content' can be taken here as coming to the same thing. Thus he says, "When a sentence contains an irreducible metaphor, it follows at once that the sentence is devoid of cognitive meaning, that it is unintelligible, that it fails to make a genuine assertion."[13]

In an interesting historical remark Edwards notes that Berkeley's objection to Locke's talk about an unknowable, material substratum that "supports" sense-qualities amounted to the claim that Locke's talk was unintelligible,

---

11 W. T. Stace, *Mysticism and Philosophy* (New York: J. B. Lippincott, 1960), p. 293.

12 Edwards, *Mind*, p. 199.   13 *Ibid.*, pp. 199–200.

involving the irreducible metaphor "supports."[14] Edwards then proceeds to suggest ways in which Locke could have answered Berkeley's objection. The second way Edwards suggests is very pertinent to his claim that Tillich's talk of being-itself involves "irreducible metaphors." I quote it in full:

A second line of defense would begin by admitting that the material substratum *would* be completely unknowable, if sensory observation were the only method of becoming acquainted with objective realities. In fact, however, it would be said, we possess a "super-sensuous" faculty with which we "experience" such realities as material and spiritual substances. We could, if we wanted, introduce a set of terms as the symbols literally referring to the data disclosed by this super-sensuous faculty and we could exchange information about these with all who share in the possession of the faculty. If we call this the "intellectual language", then, so this defense of Locke would run, sentences with metaphors when containing terms from the "sensory level", can be translated into sentences in the intellectual language which will be free from metaphors.[15]

Edwards here appears to hold that so long as the referent of our metaphorical descriptions is something we *experience,* our metaphorical descriptions are not irreducible because, he argues, we could, if we wanted, introduce some terms as literally referring to what is experienced. Hence, we could then translate our metaphorical statements into statements involving these new terms. It is, I think, doubtful that Edwards is right about this point. But what, perhaps, is more important for our purpose is that if he is right, then so far as Tillich's view is concerned it follows that Tillich's metaphorical descriptions of being-itself are *not* irreducible. For, as we have seen, Tillich surely

---

[14] *Ibid.*, p. 200.   [15] *Ibid.*, pp. 200–201.

holds that we do experience the ultimate, being-itself. In fact, it is a rather fundamental claim in his ontology that man has an immediate awareness of what is ontologically ultimate, being-itself. Surprisingly, Edwards seems completely unaware of this rather fundamental claim in Tillich. Indeed, he succeeds in getting Tillich exactly wrong when he attributes to him the view that ". . . Being-itself is, even in principle, inaccessible to anybody's observation."[16] In fact, once Tillich's actual position—that being-itself is experienced—is recognized, it follows *on Edwards' view* that Tillich's metaphors are *not* irreducible and, therefore, that Edwards' conclusion is erroneous.

But, is Edwards' view that metaphorical descriptions of what is experienced are *reducible* metaphors correct? Although this question cannot be pursued here, we must at least note that it is not obviously correct; indeed, views opposed to it are currently held by some philosophers of language. Alston, for example, argues that not only God but also many of our inner feelings—which obviously meet Edwards' condition of being experienced—are such that their metaphorical descriptions are irreducible in the sense that what they express cannot be expressed in literal terms.[17] So far as statements about God are concerned, Tillich would certainly agree with Alston. And if Alston is right concerning our inner feelings, then we have *prima facie* grounds, at least, for rejecting not only Edwards' view but also the semantic principle which states that a symbolic or metaphorical statement is meaningful only if its cognitive content is expressible by some literal statement.

---

16 *Ibid.*, p. 201. It is clear from the context that Edwards does not intend to restrict "observation" to sensory experience.

17 Alston, *Philosophy of Language*, pp. 103–6.

In the past few pages I have been concerned mainly to argue (1) that Tillich's own view is that religious statements about God are to be interpreted in terms of ontological statements about being-itself, (2) that Tillich's own view implies that the ontological statements about being-itself, as well as the religious statements about God they purport to interpret, are *irreducible* symbolic statements, and (3) that Tillich's theory is, therefore, inconsistent with the principle that a symbolic statement is meaningful only if its cognitive content is expressible by some literal statement.

Before we return to our account of primary religious symbols, one final problem needs discussion. Since statements about being-itself are, on Tillich's view, irreducible symbolic statements, and since he proposes to interpret religious statements about God in terms of ontological statements about being-itself, the question arises as to how the ontological statements can perform the job of explanation and interpretation that Tillich assigns to them. Since they too are symbolic it would seem that they are as much in need of elucidation as the theological statements about God they purport to interpret. In discussing a criticism by Alston, I suggested that even though the ontological statements are symbolic, the symbols they employ may serve a different purpose than the symbols employed in the religious statements which the ontological statements interpret. That is, if our purpose is to arrive at a conceptual grasp of the nature of ultimate reality, the symbols occurring in the ontological statements may be better suited to serve this purpose than the symbols occurring in the corresponding religious statements about God. Thus, from the vantage point of this purpose it may not be true that the symbolic ontological statements are as much in need of elucidation as the religious statements they purport to elucidate.

What Tillich is committed to holding is that a proposed explication of a religious symbol or myth need not be completely nonsymbolic in order to be an intelligible interpretation of that symbol or myth. However, it is consistent with this to hold that the interpretation must be *less symbolic* than the symbol or myth it interprets. And it is important to note that Tillich is sufficiently aware of the problem we are discussing to point out that although his ontological interpretations are symbolic, they are less symbolic than the data they interpret. Thus we have here a second reason why it may not be true that the symbolic, ontological statements are as much in need of elucidation as the religious statements they purport to interpret. We shall return to, and document, this point when we discuss Tillich's account of religious myths.

We have been considering the religious symbols Tillich classifies as transcendent level primary symbols. That is, we have been considering (*a*) God himself, (*b*) the attributes and qualities of God, and (*c*) the actions of God. These symbols do seem to satisfy Tillich's characterization of transcendent level, primary symbols, for they would normally be thought of as transcending the empirical level (thus they are transcendent level symbols) and they point directly to being-itself (thus they are primary symbols). Primary symbols on the immanent level are those which Tillich describes as "the appearances of the divine in time and space." It is clear that he means here all the finite objects that have become sacred objects by virtue of being experienced as embodying the quality of the divine. Thus, when they become objects of ultimate concern, the nation, Christ, sacred trees, etc., become immanent level, primary symbols. These symbols, like the transcendent level symbols, all point to being-itself. They differ from the transcendent level symbols by virtue of being within time and space. They are needed, Tillich suggests, in order to overcome the remoteness of the divine in the transcendent level symbols (TC, 64).

In addition to the "incarnations of the divine"—e.g., Christ and Buddha—Tillich mentions two other sets of immanent level, primary symbols; namely, "sacramental symbols" and a group he calls "sign-symbols". Sacramental symbols are natural objects which become the bearer of the holy "in a special way and under special circumstances" (TC, 64). The materials of the Lord's Supper fall into this group of symbols. By saying they are symbolic Tillich means, of course, to assert that the holy is experienced, on special occasions, as embodied in this material. He does not mean that they merely represent and remind us of something else, the body and blood of Christ. For if they only did that they would be signs, not symbols. We must, then, distinguish between regarding the materials of the Lord's Supper as religious symbols, and regarding them as religious signs. Indeed, it is in terms of this distinction that Tillich understands the famous discussion between Luther and Zwingli in Marburg in 1529. "Luther wanted to maintain the genuinely symbolic character of the elements, but Zwingli said that the sacramental materials, bread and wine, are 'only symbolic'. Thus Zwingli meant that they are only signs pointing to a story of the past" (TC, 64). It is clear that Tillich sides with Luther, and not Zwingli.

About "sign-symbols" Tillich says:

Many things—like special parts of the Church building, like the candles, like the water at the entrance of the Roman Church, like the cross in all Churches, especially Protestant Churches—were originally only signs, but in use became symbols; call them sign-symbols, signs which have become symbols (TC, 65).

We have, then, four classes of primary symbols, the first class belonging on the transcendent level, the other three on the immanent level. In outline form we may represent Tillich's classification as follows:

Primary religious symbols:

1. Transcendent (e.g., God, his attributes and actions)
2. Immanent
   a) Incarnations of the divine (e.g., Christ, Buddha)
   b) Sacramental (e.g., the materials in the Lord's Supper)
   c) Sign-Symbols (e.g., the Crucifix, the Baptismal water)

Perhaps we should observe that sacramental and sign-symbols are alike in that they tend to be conceptually dependent on symbols grouped under "incarnations of the divine." One could not explain the symbolic character of the bread and wine in the Lord's Supper, nor could one explain the significance of the Crucifix, without reference to Christ. Thus symbols grouped under "incarnations of the divine" seem to be more basic religious symbols than those grouped under "sacramental" or "sign-symbols." A similar relation of dependence seems to hold between incarnation symbols and transcendent level symbols. But these differences are, for Tillich, overshadowed by what he regards as the fundamental common feature exhibited by the symbols of these different groups—namely, their being bearers of the holy, their being objects which are experienced as embodying the quality of ultimacy. It is this feature which leads Tillich to call them "primary religious symbols," symbols that point directly to being-itself.

Having examined Tillich's view of the nature of a religious symbol and his proposed classification of these symbols, we may now consider his account of religious *myths.* The connection between myths and symbols is an intimate one, for myths arise, so Tillich thinks, when our symbolic statements about God are united into "stories" about the divine. Thus the isolated occurrence of the statement "God created the heavens and the earth" involves the use of symbolic language but, presumably, does not constitute a myth. The biblical story of the creation, however, not only involves the use of symbols, it is a myth. Thus Tillich says, "Myths are symbols of faith combined in stories about divine-human encounters" (DF, 49). Other examples of biblical myths, in Tillich's use of 'myth', are the stories concerning Paradise, the fall of Adam, the great flood, the virgin birth of the Messiah, his resurrection and ascension, etc. To speak of these stories as 'myths' is, of course, to imply that they are not *literally* true, or, at least, that the question of their literal truth or falsehood is irrelevant to their religious significance. This follows from the fact that myths—at least in those parts of the stories which are about God—are composed of sentences which are symbolic. That they must be so composed follows from Tillich's claim that we can talk about God only in language that is used symbolically.

Analogous to what we discovered in discussing theological statements, we must recognize that Tillich's rejection of literalism concerning myths is not based on the claim that contradictions arise if we (1) interpret the biblical stories in question literally and (2) regard God as an infinite, immaterial, omnipotent, omniscient, perfectly good being. He is not pointing out, for example, that a contradiction arises if we use "walked" literally in the sentence "God (an immaterial being) walked in the garden in the cool of the day." Even if a literal understanding of the activities of God as described in the biblical stories could be made consistent with the conception of God as a supreme being, Tillich would still insist that the biblical stories are to be understood *symbolically* (i.e., as myths). For the conception of God as a supreme being is for Tillich, as we have seen, a symbol for God (being-itself). Hence, Tillich's rejection of literalism is based on the fact that the presupposition of the literal understanding of the biblical stories is that God is a supreme being. As he puts it, "The presupposition of such literalism is that God is a being, acting in time and space, dwelling in a special place, affecting the course of events and being affected by them like any other being in the universe" (DF, 52).

There are, I believe, two basic difficulties in Tillich's general view of myths. Both of these difficulties were discussed in connection with his account of religious symbols, but it will be instructive to consider them again as they emerge in his discussion of myths. We may, as we did in discussing his view of symbols, present the first difficulty in the form of an argument leading to a conclusion that is certainly unacceptable to Tillich. The difficulty arises from the fact that for Tillich "symbolic language alone is able to express the ultimate." This being so it is impossible to give a nonsymbolic interpretation of what a myth says about the ultimate, God. And this is tantamount to saying that it is impossible to interpret a myth. But if I cannot interpret or explain a myth, it makes no sense to say that I understand it. Hence, on Tillich's theory it seems that no religious myth can be understood by anyone. This conclusion, of course, is unacceptable to Tillich. We must now see how it can be avoided.

Tillich's reply to the argument just sketched would, I think, take the following line. First, he would admit that one cannot be said to understand a myth unless he can interpret it and, moreover, interpret it correctly. This would seem to be a truism about symbols generally. For example, one could hardly be said to understand the Elizabethan symbol of the weeping willow unless one could interpret it correctly as representing, say, unhappy love. Second, Tillich would, I believe, admit that the proposed interpretation cannot be symbolic in the same degree as the myth itself. The difficulty, however, is that any interpretation of a religious myth cannot be completely nonsymbolic, since it could not then be about God, being-itself. His move here, it seems, is to provide an interpretation that is *less* symbolic than the myth it interprets, but not completely nonsymbolic. Finally, he would argue that a proposed explication of a myth need not be completely nonsymbolic in order to be an intelligible interpretation of the myth. It will be helpful to examine these points in connection with Tillich's discussion of a particular myth, the myth of Adam's fall.

On Tillich's view it is, of course, a mistake to understand the biblical story of the fall of Adam as a literal account of a sequence of events that happened "once upon a time" to a particular man, Adam. Instead, we must interpret the story of Adam's fall ". . . as a symbol for the human situation universally" (ST, 2:29). If so, just what does the story of the fall *symbolize* about the human situation? The fact that Tillich endeavors to answer this question indicates, I think, that he recognizes that the myth cannot be understood unless it is interpreted. At any rate, he does offer an interpretation of the fall. The interpretation is given in philosophical terms. Moreover, he argues that although the interpretation is not completely nonsymbolic, it is, nevertheless, less symbolic than the myth itself. Thus he says:

. . . the phrase "transition from essence to existence" is used in this system. It is, so to speak, a "half-way demythologization" of the myth of the Fall. The element of "once upon a time" is removed. But the demythologization is not complete, for the phrase "transition from essence to existence" still contains a temporal element. And if we speak in temporal terms about the divine, we speak in mythical terms, even if such abstract concepts as "essence" and "existence" replace mythological states and figures. Complete demythologization is not possible when speaking about the divine (ST, 2:29).

It is clear from this passage that the phrase "transition from essence to existence" is a part of Tillich's interpretation of the myth of the fall of Adam. It is also clear that although he regards the phrase as less symbolic than the story, or aspect of the story, it interprets, the phrase is still symbolic, since it contains a "temporal element." Finally, it is clear that Tillich does not think it possible for a correct interpretation of the myth to be completely nonsymbolic— this is implied by his remark, "Complete demythologization is not possible when speaking about the divine." Since he obviously regards himself as providing an interpretation of the fall of Adam, it follows that he is committed to the position that a proposed explication of a myth need not be completely nonsymbolic in order to be an intelligible interpretation of that myth. From our earlier discussion of religious statements, this is precisely what we should expect Tillich to hold.

The second basic difficulty in Tillich's view of myths arises when we consider the interpretation that Tillich gives of the myth of the fall of Adam. The difficulty with this "interpretation" (as with many of Tillich's "interpretations") is that it itself seems to require interpretation or explanation. That is, one's immediate response to the supposedly explanatory phrase "transition from essence to existence" can only be to ask what it means. The reason this is so is that Tillich invariably "translates" religious myths and traditional doctrines into statements involving highly metaphysical terms such as 'essence,' 'existence,' 'ground of being,' 'structure of being,' 'nonbeing,' 'finite freedom,' etc. As a result, the plain religious man has very little chance of understanding the myth of the fall. He does not have the background in classical metaphysics necessary for understanding its interpretation. But if the religious man does not, perhaps cannot, explain what the myth of the fall of Adam represents, what sense can we make of the claim that the story of Adam's fall functions as a *symbol* for him? Can I say that the willow tree functions as a symbol for me if I do not have a clue as to what it symbolizes, if I cannot explain or understand what I take it to be a symbol of? If *x* can function as a *symbol* for me only if I can explain what *x* symbolizes; then, since the religious man untutored in classical philosophy and theology cannot explain what, on Tillich's theory, the story of the fall symbolizes, must we not conclude that for this man the story of the fall of Adam does not function as a symbol of the transition from essence to existence? If so, then it would seem unlikely that the story of the fall could ever symbolize for the religious community, short of the members of that community undertaking the study of classical metaphysics, what Tillich regards as symbolized by the story.

The difficulty we have hit upon can be expressed in the following way. Consider the two statements: (1) For ordinary religious men the story of the fall functions as a symbol of the transition from essence to existence. (2) Ordinary religious men are unable to specify what the story of the fall symbolizes. Tillich's theory of religious myths and symbols seems to imply that both 1 and 2 are true. The problem for Tillich is to show how it is *possible* for both statements to be true. In dealing with essentially the same problem earlier, I argued that it is not a general truth that x can function as a symbol of y for someone only if he can specify y as what x symbolizes. Apart from pursuing this suggestion, I can see no way out of this difficulty that does not involve substantial changes in Tillich's theory itself.

We have had a look at what I believe are the two basic difficulties inherent in Tillich's theory of religious symbols, particularly as these problems arise in his discussion of myths. In the final paragraphs of this chapter, I shall expand the discussion of Tillich's interpretation of the myth of the fall and raise a question concerning its *consistency*.

The fall, as we have seen, is a myth which, for Tillich, depicts the transition from essence to existence, from essential man to estranged man under the conditions of existence. Adam before the fall represents man in his essential nature, in unity with God. This Tillich speaks of as the "good creation." Adam after the fall represents man in his existential predicament, estranged from his essential nature, subject to the self-destructive structures of estrangement. The actual fall represents the transition from essential manhood to existential estrangement. The story has a *temporal* setting which Tillich denies. That is, that man has fallen from his nature and is subject to the self-destructive forces of his estrangement is not a description of temporal events that happened in the life of the first man, Adam, or in the life of each man. Estrangement is a description of the *state* of existing man; it is, in some sense, the very condition present in every moment of a man's life.

. . . the transition from essence to existence is a universal quality of finite being. It is not an event of the past; for it ontologically precedes everything that happens in time and space. It sets the conditions of spatial and temporal existence (ST, 2:36).

This passage, as well as others, suggests, if not claims, that "to exist as a man" and "to be estranged from one's essential nature" are either *equivalent* or the second is *presupposed* by the first. However, in spite of this, Tillich argues, as all theologians have done, that man is *responsible* for his state of estrangement from God. Adam freely chose to transgress God's commandment and eat of the forbidden fruit. Tillich interprets this by claiming that the transition from essence to existence is mediated by *finite freedom*. In this way he claims that estrangement is not only a part of universal destiny, but is also to be viewed as the result of our finite freedom—hence, man is responsible for his estrangement from his essential nature. Thus Tillich wants to view estrangement both as a condition of existence (in this way it is a tragic feature of man's destiny) and as a result of the exercise of our finite freedom (in this way man is responsible for his estrangement).

> The meaning of the myth is that the very constitution of existence implies the transition from essence to existence. The individual act of existential estrangement is not the isolated act of an individual; it is an act of freedom which is imbedded, nevertheless, in the universal destiny of existence. . . . Every ethical decision is an act of individual freedom and of universal destiny. . . . Existence is rooted both in ethical freedom and in tragic destiny. If the one or the other side is denied, the human situation becomes incomprehensible. Their unity is the great problem of the doctrine of man (ST, 2:38).

In this statement Tillich claims that existing man is inevitably estranged, yet he is responsible for his estrangement. The question I wish to raise is whether Tillich is able to accommodate this seeming contradiction. How can man, through freedom, be held responsible for his inevitable estrangement, an apparent consequence of Tillich's ontology?[18]

In classical Christian theology the problem was to reconcile divine predestination and human freedom, original sin and individual responsibility for sin. In Tillich, the problem is to reconcile what looks like a structure of existence, estrangement, and individual responsibility for our estrangement. Tillich recognizes that we are responsible for our estrangement only if it results from our free decision—hence, his claim that "the transition from essence to existence is mediated by finite freedom." However, this phrase seems unintelligible when placed alongside assertions which imply that estrangement is a *condition* of existence.

---

[18] Reinhold Niebuhr discusses this difficulty in his essay "Biblical Thought and Ontological Speculation," included in *The Theology of Paul Tillich*, pp. 216–27. Also see Tillich's reply, pp. 342–44.

It seems unintelligible because only if man *exists* can he make a decision—hence, estrangement seems to be a condition for making a decision, not a result of a free decision. If estrangement is a condition for making a free decision, one cannot very well freely decide whether to be estranged or not.

Tillich does seem to recognize that there is a problem in his interpretation of the fall. Thus he raises the question whether his interpretation makes sin a matter of ontological necessity rather than a matter of personal responsibility and guilt (ST, 2:43). His answer is inadequate.

If God creates here and now, everything he has created participates in the transition from essence to existence. He creates the newborn child; but, if created, it falls into the state of existential estrangement. This is the point of coincidence of creation and the Fall. But it is not a logical coincidence; for the child, upon growing into maturity, affirms the state of estrangement in acts of freedom which imply responsibility and guilt (ST, 2:44).

I say that Tillich's answer is inadequate because he seems to think that the difficulty is resolved if we remember that existence, and estrangement, cannot be logically derived from essence, the structures of being; for if it were derived then God in the very act of creating would, logically, produce the state of estrangement. If this were so, then man could not be responsible for estrangement since it would be a logical consequence of the ontological structures of being. But existence cannot be logically derived from essence: ". . . theology must insist that the leap from essence to existence is the original fact—that it has the character of a leap and not of structural necessity. In spite of its tragic universality, existence cannot be derived from essence" (ST, 2:44). Now all this is beside the point if the problem is to reconcile how man can be responsible for what is a *condition* of his existence; namely, his estrangement from his essential nature. To say that the state of estrangement is not entailed by the state of essence is inadequate, perhaps irrelevant, if the problem is how man can be responsible for what is entailed by the state of existence. Thus, so far as I can determine, there is an *inconsistency* in Tillich's interpretation of the myth of the fall of Adam.[19]

---

[19] My criticism presupposes that only if man exists (or is actual) can he make a decision. If Tillich denied this presupposition he would, thereby, avoid the inconsistency I have pointed out. However, he would then have to show how it is conceptually possible for a purely potential being to make a free decision.

☙VII❧

Religion and Truth

IF A POLITICAL movement, such as communism or fascism, and a goal, such as success, can, no less than Christ or Buddha, be a *religious symbol* simply by virtue of being the focus of ultimate concern, it is clear that some distinction must be made between true religious faith and false faith, between genuine religious symbols and idolatrous symbols. In short, it is clear that Tillich must provide criteria for judging the worth of various religious faiths (ultimate concerns). Our task in this final chapter is twofold: to explicate what Tillich means when he uses the expression 'truth' in connection with religion, and to examine his attempt to establish criteria for determining the truth and value of a religious faith.

Perhaps the best way to get at what Tillich means when he speaks of a religious faith as 'true' is to consider his views concerning the possible implications of scientific truth, historical truth, and philosophical truth for the question of religious truth. The truth of faith, he says, ". . . is different from the meaning of truth in each of these ways of knowledge. Nevertheless, it is truth they all try to reach, truth in the sense of the 'really real' received adequately by the cognitive function of the human mind" (DF, 80). Since faith, as well as science, history, and philosophy, attempts to get at the truth, the 'really real' and express it adequately, Tillich concludes that ". . . we must ask what the meaning of truth in faith is, what its criteria are, and how it is related to other forms of truth with other kinds of criteria" (DF, 81). Let us look first at his view of the possible relations between scientific truth and religious truth.

Tillich is well aware of the historical conflict between science and religion, a conflict which began over the nature of things most remote from man and, then, gradually shifted to what was nearer. Thus religion and science first collided over the question of whether the earth or the sun was the center of the solar system. Next, the battle was waged over the age of the earth, and then over man's history on the earth—the conflict over evolution. Finally, man's innermost self has become the subject of dispute between religion and the youthful science, psychology. Concerning the entire conflict between religion and the sciences (astronomy, geology, biology, and psychology) Tillich has several interesting points to make. His main theme, however, can be put very simply: "scientific truth and the truth of faith do not belong to the same dimension of meaning" (DF, 81). From this central theme it follows that there can be no conflict between science and religious faith. "Science can conflict only with science, and faith only with faith; science which remains science cannot conflict with faith which remains faith" (DF, 82). But if this is so, how are we to interpret the historical conflict between science and religious faith? Tillich's answer is that the conflict has resulted from a *distortion,* either of faith or of science, or of both. That is, the conflict is due either to

(a) a conflict between science and a faith which has ceased to be faith because it has lapsed into making claims which fall in the dimension of science or to (b) a conflict between faith and a science which has ceased to be simply science and has lapsed into a faith. Sometimes the conflict is due both to a lapse of faith into science and to a lapse of science into faith.

An example of the way in which Tillich understands the conflict between science and faith may serve to make his view clear.

When the representatives of faith impeded the beginning of modern astronomy they were not aware that the Christian symbols, although using the Aristotelian-Ptolemaic astronomy, were not tied up with this astronomy. Only if the symbols of "God in heaven" and "man on earth" and "demons below the earth" are taken as descriptions of places, populated by divine or demonic beings can modern astronomy conflict with the Christian faith (DF, 82).

When faith takes its symbols—religious statements concerning God as being in heaven, or above the earth, etc.,— to have implications for astronomy, a conflict, of course, may result and historically one did result. But this was a conflict in which, on Tillich's view, faith was distorted. The conflict was possible only because the religious statements were misinterpreted and distorted by biblical literalism. The presupposition of Tillich's view here is clear. It is that religious discourse, when properly seen in its symbolic character, has no implications for the statements of science which purport to describe "the structures and relations in the universe, in so far as they can be tested by experiment and calculation in quantitative terms" (DF, 81). This presupposition should not surprise us since, as we saw in discussing Tillich's theory of religious symbols, religious statements about God and man do not have as their function the task of describing things within the universe; rather, they say something about being-itself and the meaning of being-itself for man. Since being-itself is not an item within the universe of things, religious statements, on Tillich's view, cannot come into conflict with the statements of science. This is true, Tillich maintains, even if science denies the existence of the soul.

When faith speaks of the ultimate dimension in which man lives, and in which he can win or lose his soul, or of the ultimate meaning of his existence, it is not interfering at all with the scientific rejection of the concept of the soul. A psychology without soul cannot deny this nor can a psychology with soul confirm it. The truth of man's eternal meaning lies in a dimension other than the truth of adequate psychological concepts (DF, 84).

Sometimes, Tillich argues, the conflict between religion and science is due, not to a distortion of faith (as in the example from astronomy), but to a distortion of science, to a lapse of science into a rival faith. His most plausible example of the latter is the conflict between religion and depth psychology.

Contemporary analytic or depth psychology has in many instances conflicted with pre-theological and theological expressions of faith. It is, however, not difficult in the statements of depth psychology to distinguish the more or less verified observations and hypotheses from assertions about man's nature and destiny which are clearly expressions of faith. The naturalistic elements which Freud carried from the nineteenth into the twentieth century, his basic puritanism with respect to love, his pessimism about culture, and his reduction of religion to ideological projection are all expressions of faith and not the result of scientific analysis (DF, 84).

I suspect that only the most unrepentant Freudians would deny Tillich's general point in this passage, as only the most unrepentant positivists would deny that a good deal of Freud's theory concerning neurosis and personality development is within the domain of science. Freud's works on religion and culture (*The Future of Religion, Totem and Taboo, Moses and Monotheism, Civilization and Its Discontents*) do, I believe, result as much from Freud's peculiar presuppositions of faith as from scientific analysis. There is, of course, nothing wrong with this—so long as the expressions of faith do not masquerade as the results of science. Tillich remarks:

> There is no reason to deny to a scholar who deals with man and his predicament the right to introduce elements of faith. But if he attacks other forms of faith in the name of scientific psychology, as Freud and many of his followers do, he is confusing dimensions. In this case those who represent another kind of faith are justified in resisting these attacks (DF, 84).

We have noted that whatever he means by the phrase 'the truth of faith' Tillich maintains that it cannot be refuted by the truths of science, and this because "scientific truth and the truth of faith do not belong to the same dimension of meaning." Having pressed this point, Tillich is careful to draw the corollary that scientific truth cannot establish religious truth. "The truth of faith cannot be confirmed by latest physical or biological discoveries—as it cannot be denied by them" (DF, 85).

The relation between historical truth and the truth of faith becomes important for those faiths whose chief symbols are historical figures. In Christianity, the problem of relating religious truth to historical truth became crucial once historical research began investigating the biblical literature and raised the question of the historical basis for the biblical picture of Jesus who is called the Christ. Suppose, for example, that historical research establishes that it is highly probable that Jesus did not perform some of the actions he is portrayed as performing in certain of the stories about him in the Synoptic Gospels. What effect should this historical skepticism about the biblical picture of Jesus have on the Christian faith? Tillich's answer to this question represents what I suppose is an extreme view among Christian theologians. For he concludes that the skeptical results of historical research should have no implication whatsoever for the Christian faith. Now this conclusion, by itself, represents no serious departure from what is certainly a major stand in traditional Christian thought. The extreme character of Tillich's answer becomes apparent only when we consider the *reason* that leads him to this conclusion. One might, after all, arrive at the same conclusion because of holding that faith itself provides a *guarantee* that the biblical portrait of Christ is historically correct. Hence, one might conclude that the skeptical results of historical research should have no influence on faith. Since faith itself guarantees the factual truths about Jesus, if historical research leads to results which conflict with these factual truths, it would only be a weakness on the part of faith, for faith to be affected by these results. Faith would simply be committed to the *denial* of the historical research that led to such skeptical results.

Tillich's reason for concluding that the skeptical results of historical research into the life of Jesus should have no influence on Christian faith is not that faith guarantees the biblical portrait of Jesus to be historically accurate. Rather, his reason for so concluding is that faith, when properly understood, makes no factual claims whatsoever about some man named 'Jesus' who flourished in the years 1 to 30. And this, I think, does represent an extreme view.

Faith, on Tillich's view, cannot be upset by historical skepticism concerning Jesus, because faith in Christ does not imply or require the truth of any factual claims about the life, character, and activities of the historical Jesus. Thus the stories about Jesus which speak of his virgin birth, his sayings (the Sermon on the Mount, etc.), his deeds (the miracles), his death on a cross, and his physical resurrection are, when taken as reports of facts and events in history, not, for Tillich, matters of faith at all.

It is not a matter of faith to decide how much legendary, mythological and historical material is amalgamated in the stories about the birth and resurrection of the Christ. It is not a matter of faith to decide which version of the reports about the early days of the Church has the greatest probability. All these questions must be decided, in terms of more or less probability, by historical research. They are questions of historical truth, not of the truth of faith (DF, 88).

In view of Tillich's extreme view concerning the *irrelevance* of factual truths about the historical Jesus for faith in Christ, it is not surprising that theologians have criticized his Christology; indeed, some have argued that his Christology is internally inconsistent. Thus one acute observer remarks:

Tillich appears to imply that Christian faith would not be affected by however great a degree of skepticism regarding the historicity of Jesus of Nazareth. Yet he makes the idea of incarnation central in his understanding of the Christian faith. But surely the idea of incarnation is a *false* idea if no incarnation actually took place on the level of ordinary history. Or to put it otherwise, how can Christ be "the center of history" if he was not himself a real historical person, but only an idea? An idea can indeed be the center of a system of ideas, but only an actual historical figure can be the center of *history*.[1]

---

[1] John Baille, "Interrogation of Paul Tillich," *Philosophical Interrogations,* ed. Sydney and Beatrice Rome (New York: Holt, Rinehart and Winston, 1964), p. 363.

I propose to consider in some detail Tillich's reply to this criticism since it will require us to supplement the account of Tillich's view I gave above, and will also enlarge our understanding of what Tillich means by the expression "truth of faith." In his reply he refers to the development of his Christology in *Systematic Theology* 2 and remarks:

Nothing is more emphasized in these chapters than the factual side of the event on which Christianity is based. But I ask the question, How can the factual element be cognitively reached so that it gives the basis for the Christian faith? And the answer is: *Not* through scholarly research in the sources, a procedure which in spite of all its great *indirect* merits can produce no more than changing degrees of probability, and which would make the faith of the church dependent on the hermeneutic skills of a group of highly specialized scholars. Instead of that, I suggest that the participation of the faith of the church and its individual member guarantees the event which has transformed old being into new being in them. This experience always was and still is the basis for the certainty that "eternal God-manhood" has appeared in a personal life under the conditions of estrangement without being conquered by them. This event is rightly called the center of history.[2]

I argued that Tillich's view is that none of the qualities and deeds attributed to Jesus in the New Testament can be matters of faith in so far as they are considered as descriptions of an historical person who flourished in the first century of our era. If this is Tillich's view, as I think it is, the question naturally arises as to whether faith in Christ, on his view, has any connection whatever with a historical person. Tillich's reply to the criticism quoted above makes it clear that Christian faith is, for him, connected with the life of some historical person—it does not matter whether he bore the name 'Jesus' or some other name—and even

---

[2] *Ibid.*, p. 364.

guarantees some very general description as being true of that person. It is this historical person who is the Christ and the center of history.

Faith in Christ, then, guarantees—even for Tillich—a factual truth. For faith guarantees *the existence of a historical person of a certain sort.* The vital question, of course, is: what *sort* of person is it whose existence, presumably in the first century, is guaranteed by the Christian faith? Tillich's formulation of his answer to this question varies, but the substance of it is clear enough. The *sort* of person whose existence faith in Christ guarantees is a person who exhibited qualities that grasped and transformed the disciples and led to the *picture* of Jesus that we have in the New Testament.

Exactly what can faith guarantee? . . . Faith itself is the immediate (not mediated by conclusions) evidence of the New Being within and under the conditions of existence. . . . It guarantees a personal life in which the New Being has conquered the old being. But it does not guarantee his name to be Jesus of Nazareth. Historical doubt concerning the existence and the life of someone with this name cannot be overruled. He might have had another name. (This is a historically absurd, but logically necessary, consequence of the historical method.) Whatever his name, the New Being was and is actual in this man (ST, 2:114).

Tillich's description of the sort of person whose existence faith guarantees is unquestionably vague. It is vague in the sense that it does not *specify* what qualities that person had in virtue of which the disciples were grasped and transformed in their encounter with him. Was he very intelligent? Was he a morally good man? Perhaps he was a charmer and a deceiver who mystified the disciples into believing he was sent from God. Perhaps he felt superior to his friends and despised those who disagreed with his opinions. Could he have been a murderer? One naturally feels that if faith in Christ is to mean anything at all, it must preclude the ascription of at least some *specific attributes* to the historical figure whom the disciples apparently knew by the name 'Jesus'. But Tillich remains silent on such matters. He remains silent, I think, because he wishes to hold the view that historical research is the *only* avenue to knowledge of the factual truths concerning events and personalities in the past. Religious truth is no more to be confused with historical truth than it is with scientific truth. Holding this view, Tillich sees that if faith were committed to a particular historical biography of Jesus, whether the one presented in the Bible or some other, faith would be *dependent* on the results of historical research. Tillich finds this objectionable. "Faith cannot rest on such unsure ground" (ST, 2:113). That is, historical research can at best provide probability, but faith requires certainty. Hence, faith cannot be made to depend on the results of historical research. Once this is granted, if it is also admitted that historical research is the only avenue to our knowledge of facts concerning the past, we are led to the view that faith in Christ cannot imply the ascription of any specific traits to the person in whom the disciples encountered the New Being.

More traditionally minded theologians might agree with Tillich that historical research yields only probabilities. But they undoubtedly would reject the view that such research is our only avenue to knowledge of factual truths concerning the past. Faith, in their view, guarantees the existence of Jesus of Nazareth and at least the essentials in the biblical picture—in particular, his death on the cross and his bodily resurrection.[3]

Perhaps realizing that Christian faith requires a more solid historical foundation than is afforded by his vague description of the man encountered by the disciples, Tillich argues that there must be an *analogy* between the New Testament picture of Jesus and the historical figure met by the disciples.

No special trait of this picture can be verified with certainty. But it can be definitely asserted that through this picture the New Being has power to transform those who are transformed by it. This implies that there is an *analogia imaginis,* namely, an analogy between the picture and the actual personal life from which it has arisen. It was this reality, when encountered by the disciples, which created the picture. And it was, and still is, this picture which mediates the transforming power of the New Being (ST, 2:115).

This suggestion by Tillich is helpful. If it were worked out more fully perhaps one would be justified in precluding the ascription of certain features to the man encountered by the disciples, features such as being a murderer, being hateful, and the like. But, of course, once this is done, it would seem to follow that faith can guarantee some specific factual truths concerning the historical Jesus. And this conflicts with Tillich's basic conviction that historical research is the only avenue to factual truths of a specific nature concerning past events and persons. I conclude that

---

[3] Although Tillich thinks it highly probable that Jesus died on a cross, his description of what faith guarantees as a factual truth concerning the death of the historical person behind the New Testament picture does not imply that he died on a cross. Concerning the story of the cross he remarks: "The only factual element in it having the immediate certainty of faith is the surrender of him who is called the Christ to the ultimate consequence of existence, namely, death under the conditions of estrangement. Everything else is a matter of historical probability, elaborated out of legendary interpretation" (ST, 2: 155).

there is an unresolved tension in Tillich's thought between what he feels to be the historical demands of Christian faith and what he takes to be the proper way in which man obtains knowledge concerning specific factual truths about the past. The tension, I believe, becomes apparent in his discussion of faith and historical skepticism concerning Jesus.

We have seen that whatever Tillich means by a truth of faith, he is anxious to distinguish such truth from both scientific truth and historical truth. On the whole his view is that religious truth has little to do with truth in science or history. "Neither scientific nor historical truth can affirm or negate the truth of faith. The truth of faith can neither affirm nor negate scientific or historical truth" (DF, 89). We must now briefly consider his view concerning the relation between philosophical truth and religious truth.

Tillich conceives of philosophy as an inquiry concerning the nature of reality as a whole. That is, unlike the sciences, philosophy does not study the features of one particular realm or dimension of reality; philosophy tries to discover the most general features of reality as such, features which are exhibited in every realm of being. Again, unlike science and history, there is a point at which philosophy and faith share a common subject matter; namely, ultimate reality. It is this point which makes the relation of faith to philosophy different from the relation of faith to science and history.

Philosophical truth is truth about the structure of being; the truth of faith is truth about one's ultimate concern. Up to this point the relation seems to be very similar to that between the truth of faith and scientific truth. But the difference is that there is a point of identity between the ultimate of the philosophical question and the ultimate of the religious concern. In both cases ultimate reality is sought and expressed—conceptually in philosophy, symbolically in religion. Philosophical truth consists in true concepts concerning the ultimate; the truth of faith consists in true symbols concerning the ultimate (DF, 90–91).

This passage contains two important points. First, Tillich indicates what is meant by 'truth of faith' or 'religious truth.' We have seen that religious truth is not be confused with scientific or historical truth. Here we learn that "the truth of faith consists in true symbols concerning the ultimate." What this means, I think, is that a faith is true just in case its symbols are true symbols of the ultimate. Second, Tillich claims that both philosophy and faith concern themselves with ultimate reality, the former in terms of concepts, the latter in terms of symbols. The first of these two points will be elaborated when we discuss Tillich's concept of idolatry. For the moment we must concentrate our attention on the second point.

Although both philosophy and faith seek to express ultimate reality, they approach the ultimate, Tillich argues, from fundamentally different perspectives. "The philosophical relation is in principle a detached description of the basic structure in which the ultimate manifests itself. The relation of faith is in principle an involved expression of concern about the meaning of the ultimate for the faithful" (DF, 91). Presumably, these different perspectives from which ultimate reality is approached account for the fact that philosophy expresses itself in *concepts* concerning the ultimate; whereas, faith expresses itself in *symbols* concerning the ultimate. Thus, even though philosophy and faith share a common subject-matter, they are in principle quite different. But this is only *in principle*. In practice, Tillich maintains, faith and philosophy are much closer together than our remarks thus far have indicated. The main reason for this—Tillich gives several—is that the concepts in which philosophy expresses the ultimate are not altogether free of symbolic elements, and the symbols in which faith expresses the ultimate ". . . have conceptual elements which can and must be developed as soon as philosophical consciousness has appeared" (DF, 95).

In the idea of God the concepts of being, life, spirit, unity and diversity are implied. In the symbol of the creation concepts of finitude, anxiety, freedom and time are implied. The symbol of the "fall of Adam" implies a concept of man's essential nature, of his conflict with himself, or his estrangement from himself. Only because every religious symbol has conceptual potentialities is "theology" possible (DF, 95).

The fact that religious symbols have conceptual potentialities makes it possible for the theologian to elucidate religious statements about the ultimate in terms of ontological statements about the ultimate. In Tillich's system, as we saw, religious statements using the symbol *God* are elucidated in terms of ontological statements using the concept *being-itself*. The fact that philosophical concepts are not completely free of symbolic elements makes it impossible for ontological statements about the ultimate to be nonsymbolic. In Tillich's system this gave rise to the problem of how the ontological statements could elucidate the religious statements, since the former are also symbolic. In discussing this problem, I suggested (1) that the ontological statements are *less symbolic*—"half way demythologizations"—than the religious statements they purport to elucidate and (2) they may be better suited to the purpose of providing a conceptual grasp of the nature of ultimate reality than the corresponding religious symbols. Points 1 and 2, I argued, need to be thoroughly investigated before we conclude that because Tillich's ontological statements about the ultimate are symbolic they cannot serve to elucidate religious statements about the ultimate.

Although Tillich claims that philosophical concepts must be employed in the elucidation of the symbols of faith, he denies that philosophy can provide the criteria in terms of which the truth of faith is to be judged. His view seems to be that the "conceptual potentialities" of the symbols of faith can be developed in many different ways, depending on the particular philosophy in terms of which its symbols are elucidated. Faith does not determine that a particular philosophy is the correct philosophy. Nor can philosophy determine that one religious symbol is true, another false.

There is a philosophy implied in every symbol of faith. But faith does not determine the movement of the philosophical thought, just as philosophy does not determine the character of one's ultimate concern. Symbols of faith can open the eyes of the philosopher to qualities of the universe which otherwise would not have been recognized by him. But faith does not command a definite philosophy, although churches and theological movements have claimed and used Platonic, Aristotelian, Kantian or Humean philosophies. The philosophical implications of the symbols of faith can be developed in many ways, but the truth of faith and the truth of philosophy have no authority over each other (DF, 95).

It is clear that Tillich's position is that the conceptual analysis of the symbols of faith cannot determine the truth of that faith. And this means that we have yet to discover what it means to speak of a faith as 'true' and what the criteria are in terms of which the truth and value of a religious faith may be judged. "In what sense, then, can one speak of the truth of faith if it cannot be judged by any other kind of truth, whether scientific, historical or philosophical?" (DF, 95).

Faith, Tillich remarks, has both a subjective and an objective side. His answer to the question, "What is meant by the truth of faith?" is given for each of these two sides of faith. "From the subjective side one must say that faith is true if it adequately expresses an ultimate concern. From the objective side one must say that faith is true if its content is the really ultimate" (DF, 96).

Perhaps it will aid our inquiry if we introduce the terms 'subjectively true' and 'objectively true' and ask what these terms can mean in their application to faith. Given Tillich's remarks about the truth of faith, I think we can say what it means for a faith to be subjectively true. A faith is *subjectively true* at a given time only if at that time its symbols are the foci of ultimate concern for some group. In short, a faith is subjectively true only when its symbols are alive, not dying or dead. That this is what it means for a faith to be subjectively true is, I think, clear from the following remark Tillich makes concerning the truth of faith from its subjective side.

The relation of man to the ultimate undergoes changes. Contents of ultimate concern vanish or are replaced by others. A divine figure ceases to create reply, it ceases to be a common symbol and loses its power to move for action. Symbols which for a certain period, or in a certain place, expressed truth of faith for a certain group now only remind of the faith of the past. They have lost their truth, and it is an open question whether dead symbols can be revived. Probably not for those to whom they have died. If we look from this point of view at the history of faith, including our own period, the criterion of the truth of faith is whether or not it is alive (DF, 96–97).

The basic difficulty of understanding Tillich's idea of a *true* faith arises when we ask what can be meant by saying that a faith is objectively true. The sentence quoted above—"From the objective side one must say that faith is true if its content is the really ultimate"—is, at best, highly misleading. For he generally uses the expression "the content of faith" to refer to a religious symbol. But no symbol—a finite entity—could possibly be "the really ultimate." However, in spite of this misleading statement, there is, I think, no real problem in discovering the proper phrase Tillich wishes to employ in explaining what he means by a faith being true on its objective side, being objectively true. A faith is *objectively true* just in case it is not *idolatrous.* That the notion of idolatry is appropriate here is clear from Tillich's remark concerning the truth of faith from its objective side. "The other criterion of the truth of a symbol of faith is that it expresses the ultimate which is really ultimate. In other words, that it is not idolatrous" (DF, 97). The basic difficulty alluded to above is the problem of understanding Tillich's concept of idolatry. A thorough investigation of this concept must be undertaken, since it is the central concept in Tillich's account of true and false religious faith. It will be instructive to begin our investigation by examining in some detail a few of the statements Tillich makes in explaining his idea of idolatry.

Many of Tillich's remarks about idolatrous faith suggest that we are to understand *idolatry* as exemplified by any faith in which the object of ultimate concern is not the true ultimate. Thus he remarks: "In true faith the ultimate concern is a concern about the truly ultimate; while in idolatrous faith preliminary, finite realities are elevated to the rank of ultimacy" (DF, 12). Presumably, to elevate a finite reality to the rank of ultimacy is simply to take that finite reality, rather than the true ultimate, as the object of one's ultimate concern. This is what occurs, Tillich seems to suggest, when the nation becomes an object of ultimate concern.

There is a risk if what we considered as a matter of ultimate concern proves to be a matter of preliminary and transitory concern—as, for example, the nation. . . . The reaction of despair in people who have experienced the breakdown of their national claims is an irrefutable proof of the idolatrous character of their national concern. In the long run this is the inescapable result of an ultimate concern, the subject matter of which is not ultimate (DF, 17–18).

I shall suggest later that the remarks I have just quoted are susceptible to a different, more complicated, interpretation than the one we are now considering. Because of its simplicity, I shall call the interpretation we are now considering the "naïve conception of idolatry." According to the naïve conception we are to understand that men are ultimately concerned about many things. When a man is ultimately concerned about the true ultimate—being-itself, the ground of being—his faith is genuine. When a man is ultimately concerned about something other than the ultimate (e.g., the nation) his faith is idolatrous. We must now see why this interpretation of Tillich's concept of idolatry is naïve.

Perhaps the first difficulty that presents itself in considering this view of idolatry is that ultimate concern about Christ or Buddha, no less than about success or the nation, would be an idolatrous faith, for Christ and Buddha are also finite realities. What this difficulty makes clear is that the question of whether or not an ultimate concern is idolatrous is much more complex than the naïve conception can account for. It is not simply a matter of whether the object of one's ultimate concern is some finite reality or, as in genuine faith, the true ultimate, being-itself. That this is so follows from two assertions that, as we have seen, occupy a rather fundamental position in Tillich's philosophical theology. These assertions are: (1) every ultimate concern is concern about the ultimate, being-itself, and (2) every ultimate concern has a concrete content, some finite reality, which is the focus of that concern.

Clearly, if every ultimate concern involves both the true ultimate and some concrete content or finite reality, then we cannot say simply that idolatry occurs when the ultimate concern is concern about something finite, and genuine faith occurs when the ultimate concern is concern about the true ultimate. Or, at the very least, if we do say this we must not be led to conclude either that there is an ultimate concern that does not have as its focus something finite, or that there is an ultimate concern that is not, in some sense, a concern about the ultimate, being-itself. But, since the naïve conception does naturally lead to one or both of these conclusions, we must, if our aim is to clarify Tillich's idea of idolatry, abandon the naïve conception of idolatry.

We have been considering, thus far, the idea of idolatry as it applies to a religious faith (ultimate concern). Thus we have spoken of 'idolatrous faith' and contrasted that expression with 'genuine faith.' It will help matters, I think, if we note first that the expression 'idolatrous faith' seems to be derivative from the expression 'idolatrous symbol.' That is, I am suggesting that the question of whether or not a religious faith is idolatrous reduces, for Tillich, to the question of whether or not the concrete content—

be it nation, success, Christ, or Buddha—is idolatrous. But since the concrete content of an ultimate concern is identical with a religious symbol, it is clear that the basic idea that needs interpretation and explanation is the idea of an *idolatrous symbol.* Among symbols, of course, it is proper to apply the term 'idolatrous' only to members of the class of *religious* symbols. Once the idea of an idolatrous symbol is clarified we can simply define an "idolatrous religious faith" as any ultimate concern whose concrete content (religious symbol) is idolatrous.

As we saw in Chapter IV, an object becomes a religious symbol by virtue of being the focus of an experience of ultimate concern. In this experience the object is encountered as embodying the holy, the quality of ultimacy which, on Tillich's interpretation, is ultimate reality, being-itself. The point that we must not lose sight of is that when a religious symbol becomes idolatrous it does not cease to embody—for those who experience it with ultimate concern—the quality of ultimacy, the holy. That is, we must not think that the idolatrous symbol no longer manifests the holy to those for whom it has become an idolatrous symbol of the divine. The difference on Tillich's theory, I am arguing, between the genuine symbol and the idolatrous symbol is *not* that the former embodies the holy, and the latter no longer embodies it. That this is an incorrect view can be shown in a general way from the conclusions we arrived at in Chapter IV. There we saw that it is part of the essential nature of the religious symbol to manifest the holy to those for whom it is a religious symbol —that is, for those for whom it is the concrete content of their ultimate concern. For x to be a religious symbol for S and for x to be experienced by S as embodying the quality of the holy are, as we saw, inextricable from one another in Tillich's theory of symbolism. Now it is clear that an idolatrous symbol is a religious symbol; moreover, it must be a live religious symbol. If a religious symbol is *dead*, it no longer is the content of ultimate concern and, therefore, cannot be an idolatrous symbol. From these two considerations—namely, (1) that a religious symbol embodies the holy and (2) that an idolatrous symbol is a religious symbol—it follows that an idolatrous symbol embodies the holy, manifests being-itself to those for whom it is a symbol of the divine.

The conclusion just deduced is, I think, contained implicitly, if not explicitly, in several of Tillich's remarks. For example, after discussing idolatrous faith, he remarks:

Where there is faith there is awareness of holiness. This seems to contradict what has just been said about idolatrous faith. But it does not contradict our analysis of idolatry. It only contradicts the popular way in which the word 'holy' is used (DF, 12).

What Tillich had pointed out in his discussion of idolatrous faith was its demonic, destructive influence on those whose faith it is. The point he is emphasizing in the passage just quoted is that idolatrous faith involves, like all faith, an awareness of the presence of the divine, the holy. The "contradiction" he alludes to is between the demonic, destructive character of idolatrous faith and the popular understanding of holiness as moral perfection. In his own view there is no contradiction because holiness is understood, following Otto, as a quality of ultimacy ". . . which remains mysterious in spite of its appearance, and it exercises both an attractive and a repulsive function on those who encounter it" (DF, 13). In short, there is no contradiction because the holy can be experienced as destructive, as well as creative. Thus, for Tillich, even though idolatrous faith is demonic and destructive, we are to recognize that it still involves an awareness of the holy—that is, the idolatrous symbol still embodies and manifests the holy.

The holy which is demonic, or ultimately destructive, is identical with the content of idolatrous faith. Idolatrous faith is still faith. The holy which is demonic is still holy. This is the point where the ambiguous character of religion is most visible and the dangers of faith are most obvious: the danger of faith is idolatry and the ambiguity of the holy is its demonic possibility. Our ultimate concern can destroy us as it can heal us. But we never can be without it (DF, 16).

Since the idolatrous symbol and the genuine religious symbol both manifest the holy, we cannot use the presence or absence of the holy as a basis for distinguishing them. What, then, is it that makes a religious symbol idolatrous? Perhaps it is the way in which the symbol is thought or felt to embody the holy. That is, perhaps the idolatrous symbol is a symbol that is viewed as having the quality of the holy in a way quite different from how the genuine symbol is felt to be related to the holy. If we can make this clear, I think we will have an explanation of what it is for a symbol to be idolatrous on Tillich's theory. The passage in which Tillich most clearly develops this conception of idolatry is the following:

Holiness cannot become actual except through holy "objects." But holy objects are not holy in and of themselves. They are holy only by negating themselves in pointing to the divine of which they are the mediums. If they establish themselves as holy, they become demonic. They still are "holy," but their holiness is anti-divine. A nation which looks upon itself as holy is correct in so far as everything can become a vehicle of man's ultimate concern, but the nation is incorrect in so far as it considers itself to be inherently holy.

Innumerable things, all things in a way, have the power of becoming holy in a mediate sense. They can point to something beyond themselves. But, if their holiness comes to be considered inherent, it becomes demonic. This happens continually in the actual life of most religions. The representations of man's ultimate concern—holy objects—tend to become his ultimate concern. They are transformed into idols. Holiness provokes idolatry (ST, 1:216).

There are several points that need to be emphasized here. First, it should be absolutely clear that Tillich's view is that the idolatrous symbol does not, by virtue of being idolatrous, cease to manifest the holy. Second, we have in this passage a confirmation of the point made in earlier chapters that man encounters the holy only as a quality in finite objects. I take this to be an implication of the remark, "Holiness cannot become actual except through holy 'objects'." Third, it should be clear that what Tillich refers to here as "holy objects" are identical with the referents of the expressions "religious symbols" and "concrete contents of ultimate concern." Fourth, it seems that Tillich's view is that idolatry has to do with the *relation* between the symbol and the holy. That is, his view seems to be that when the quality of the holy which the symbol embodies and manifests is taken to be *inherent* in the symbol, then the symbol ceases to be a genuine or true religious symbol and, instead, becomes idolatrous. Apparently, then, so long as the symbol is viewed as mediating the holy, as being a vehicle through which the holy is encountered, as not having the quality of the holy in the way in which it possesses its natural properties, the symbol remains genuine. But once the symbol is viewed as having the quality of holiness inherently, and not mediately or derivatively, the symbol becomes idolatrous, it is "transformed into an idol." Finally, we must note that in describing how a symbol becomes idolatrous Tillich seems to vacillate between speaking of this as due to the symbol itself and speaking of it as due to those for whom it is a religious symbol. Thus he speaks here of symbols *establishing themselves* as holy. But he also speaks of the holiness of the symbols *being considered* inherent. And elsewhere he is careful to attribute the establishment of the symbol as inherently holy to those for whom it is a symbol. Thus in speaking of religious symbols he says, ". . . they always have the tendency (in the human mind, of course) to replace that to which they are supposed to point, and to become ultimate in themselves. And in the moment in which they do this, they become idols. All idolatry is nothing else than the absolutizing of symbols of the Holy, and making them identical with the Holy itself" (TC, 60).

There are, as we have seen, several phrases Tillich employs in describing what goes on when a symbol becomes idolatrous. Some of these phrases are misleading in that they suggest the naïve conception of idolatry discussed and abandoned earlier. It will be instructive to collect a few of the phrases together and show how they must be interpreted if we are not to misunderstand Tillich's idea of idolatry. When a religious symbol becomes idolatrous, we may say, following Tillich, that:

1. The symbol, rather than the true ultimate, has become the object of ultimate concern (DF, 12).
2. The symbol has become identical with, or replaced, that to which it points, the true ultimate (TC, 60).
3. The symbol has established itself as holy (ST, 1:216).
4. The holiness of the symbol has come to be considered inherent (ST, 1:216).

5. The symbol has been elevated to the rank of ultimacy (ST, 1:13).

6. The symbol has ceased to be transparent to the ultimate (UC, 29).

From these various descriptions of the idolatrous symbol I have selected number 4 as perhaps the most exact and clear expression of Tillich's conception of idolatry. According to this view a religious symbol may be viewed either as being *inherently* holy *or* as being holy because it points to and participates in the ultimate, being-itself. In either case the symbol manifests and embodies the quality of holiness. But in the former case the symbol is felt to have this quality inherently, not derivatively, whereas in the latter case there is an awareness that the symbol embodies the quality of holiness because it is a vehicle through which ultimate reality—which transcends everything finite, including the symbol—manifests itself.

It is in terms of this conception of idolatry that we must, to avoid misunderstanding, interpret the other descriptive phrases collected above. Since phrases 1 and 2 are perhaps the most difficult to interpret in accordance with the conception of idolatry I am elaborating, I shall concentrate on them, letting the results serve as a model for interpreting the other, less troublesome phrases. According to 1, an idolatrous symbol is a symbol that has become the object of ultimate concern. On this description genuine faith occurs when the true ultimate is the object of ultimate concern, and idolatrous faith occurs when the symbol becomes the object of ultimate concern. On the view of idolatry I am elaborating, we must interpret the situation in which the true ultimate is said to be the object of ultimate concern (genuine faith) as one in which the worshiper regards the symbol of his faith as mediating the holy to him, as a vehicle through which the true ultimate is experienced, but not as inherently holy. That this is how we must interpret this situation is, I think, clear once we recognize that on Tillich's view the true ultimate is encountered only as 'embodied' in some finite object. There is no access to the divine apart from the religious symbol.

How can we understand the description of idolatry in terms of the symbol, rather than the true ultimate, being the object of ultimate concern? My suggestion is that when the symbol is regarded as inherently holy, it is natural, even if misleading, to speak of it as being the object of ultimate concern, since it takes on a significance in the psychic life of the individual which it can never have so long as it is viewed as a vehicle of the true ultimate. When a man considers the symbol of his faith as inherently holy it is inevitable that the finite qualities of the symbol take on an infinite significance for him. The symbol itself with all its finite qualities—not just the quality of ultimacy which he experiences in connection with the symbol—is regarded as *ultimate*. The demands the symbol makes on him are uncritically received and passionately carried out because they are seen as inherently holy. Thus the implications for the life of the worshiper are profound and far-reaching when he comes to regard the symbol as inherently holy. In view of the supremacy the symbol comes to occupy in his life, I suggest that it is natural to say, as Tillich does, that the symbol, rather than the true ultimate, has become the object of his ultimate concern. It is, I have argued, also misleading to describe idolatry in this fashion.

According to description 2, an idolatrous symbol is one that has become identical with, or has replaced, that to which it points, the true ultimate. That this description of idolatry needs interpretation is, I think, fairly obvious. Clearly no symbol (finite entity) could ever actually become identical with being-itself, the metaphysical ultimate. How then are we to interpret this description of idolatry? First, I think, we must distinguish something's being psychologically ultimate from its being metaphysically ultimate. In the situation of genuine faith the metaphysical ultimate is the psychological ultimate. That is, when the worshiper views the symbol as mediating the holy to him, we can say that what is psychologically ultimate for him is not the symbol itself but the holiness it mediates. In idolatrous faith, the worshiper views the quality of holiness as inherent in the symbol and, hence, the symbol itself—with all its natural properties, not just its holiness—tends to become psychologically ultimate for him. Now, since in genuine faith the true ultimate is what is psychologically ultimate, and since in idolatrous faith the symbol itself becomes what is psychologically ultimate, it is perhaps not inappropriate to describe the symbol in idolatrous faith as *replacing* the true ultimate. For, in terms of occupying the position of being psychologically ultimate, the symbol does—in the transition from genuine to idolatrous faith—replace the true ultimate.

Perhaps Tillich's remark that the symbol, in idolatrous faith, becomes *identical* with that to which it points, the true ultimate, can be interpreted in the following way. As a matter of ontological fact, of course, the symbol cannot become the metaphysical ultimate. But in treating the symbol as supreme in his life, as psychologically ultimate, the worshiper, in idolatrous faith, *identifies* the symbol with the position and place in his life that the real ultimate occupies in genuine faith.

These suggestions as to how we may understand some of Tillich's descriptions of idolatry are, it must be acknowledged, tentative, speculative, and quite possibly incorrect. Indeed, there may be facets of Tillich's conception of idolatry that are incompatible with what I have taken to be the essential features of his theory of symbolism. But in terms of the analysis of Tillich's discussion of religious symbols that I have given, it seems that the only account of idolatry that fits the analysis is the one I have been developing. The essence of idolatry on this account is that the quality of holiness that is experienced as embodied in the symbol comes to be regarded as an inherent, intrinsic quality of the symbol, rather than as a quality the symbol manifests because of its participation in the transcendent reality, being-itself. When this occurs, the symbol—on the account I am giving—does not cease to express or point to the ultimate; rather, it expresses and points to the ultimate in an idolatrous way.

Having given an account of Tillich's concept of idolatry, we may now recapitulate our explanation of what Tillich means when he speaks of the truth of a faith. He means, as we saw, two different things, depending on whether we are viewing faith from its subjective or its objective side. I propose, therefore, to explain what he means when he speaks of a faith as *true* by introducing the expressions 'subjectively true' and 'objectively true.' A true faith is a faith that is both subjectively true and objectively true. These latter notions are elucidated as follows:

A faith is *subjectively true* just in case its symbols are

alive—i.e., are the foci of the ultimate concern for a group.

A faith is *objectively true* just in case its symbols are not idolatrous.

It should be observed that both 'subjective truth' and 'objective truth' are predicates that a faith may exhibit at one time and not at another. A faith may be subjectively true, and then lose that predicate. This has been the fate, for example, of the polytheistic faiths. They once were subjectively true, but now their symbols are dying, if not already dead. Objective truth is also something that may characterize a faith for a time, and then, for various reasons, cease to characterize it—its symbols having become idolatrous. The tendency toward idolatry is present in every genuine faith, and it seems to be Tillich's view that many faiths which once were objectively true have ceased to be so—not because their symbols have died, but because they have become idolatrous.

The weakness of all faith is the ease with which it becomes idolatrous. The human mind, Calvin has said, is a continuously working factory of idols. . . . Every type of faith has the tendency to elevate its concrete symbols to absolute validity (DF, 97).

The terms 'subjectively true' and 'objectively true' were introduced in order to clarify Tillich's discussion of faith and truth. Perhaps we should observe how these concepts are interrelated. Any faith that is subjectively true at a given time need not be objectively true at that time, for it may be idolatrous. At the time when a symbol is idolatrous for a group it is, as I argued earlier, not a dead symbol. Hence, we may conclude that if a faith is subjectively true at a given time then it is either objectively true or idolatrous at that time. Any faith that is objectively true or idolatrous at a given time must be subjectively true at that time.

For the purpose of judging and evaluating the various faiths by which men live, it should be clear that the question of the objective truth of a faith is vastly more important than the question of its subjective truth. Every faith is at some time or other subjectively true. Every religious or quasi-religious faith by which some group is now living is subjectively true. The point of speaking of a faith as 'true' on its subjective side is, Tillich notes, simply to acknowledge the truth in all religious symbols and types of faith (DF, 96). However, not every faith by which men now live is objectively true. The idea of objective truth provides a basis in terms of which man's faiths—at least those whose symbols are still alive—may be divided into two classes: the class of those which are genuine, whose symbols are transparent to the divine; and the class of those which are demonic and destructive, whose symbols are idolatrous.

Perhaps Tillich's most frequent example of a contemporary idolatrous faith is nationalism, with its idolatrous symbol, the nation. In contrast to nationalism, he surely regards Christian faith—at least in some of its forms—with its symbol, the Christ, as objectively true. It is important, however, not to misunderstand the difference between these two faiths. Unless I am mistaken, Tillich's view is that it is not *necessary* for nationalism to be idolatrous, nor is it *necessary* for Christian faith to be genuine. Each faith *can* be genuine, objectively true, and each *can* be demonic, idolatrous. That nationalism as a faith need not be idolatrous—of course, it need not even be a faith—is, I think, clearly implied in Tillich's remark about nationalism, socialism, and humanism as ultimate concerns. "If they are *really* ultimate they become demonized; if on the other hand, they are kept as manifestations of the ultimate and remain 'transparent,' then they are proper or acceptable, ethically speaking" (UC, 29). Further confirmation of this point is provided by Tillich's affirmative responses to the questions put by Professor D. Mackenzie Brown:

Professor: Dr. Tillich, are you saying that nationalism, the nation as the motherland, is a legitimate symbol of the divine—if we want to use that term—so long as we see through it and beyond it?
Dr. Tillich: Yes, exactly.
Professor: But the moment we forget that it is only a symbol or a manifestation, and begin to worship it for itself, it becomes idolatry, becomes demonic?
Dr. Tillich: Exactly (UC, 30).

The development of German nationalism into fascism marks, for Tillich, the emergence of an *idolatrous* form of the faith of nationalism.

That even the symbol of Jesus as the Christ may become idolatrous follows from the interpretation I have given of Tillich's concept of idolatry. A symbol becomes idolatrous on that interpretation when those for whom it is a religious symbol regard it as inherently holy, rather than as a vehicle of the divine. There is no reason why a Christian is not as capable of so regarding his symbol as anyone else. In fact, Tillich thinks that idolatry is a persistent and permanent danger in Christian faith (DF, 104).

It is the unavoidable possibility of idolatry that creates the element of risk in every faith and, consequently, makes courage an essential element in every act of faith. No faith —even faith in Jesus as the Christ—can provide certainty that its symbol will not, in the long run, prove to be idolatrous. The risk of faith has nothing to do with the question of the subjective truth of one's faith—this is a matter of certainty. Risk and doubt are concerned only with the question of objective truth, with the question of whether the symbol of one's faith is genuine or idolatrous. This is a matter about which certainty is simply not possible. These points are emphasized by Tillich in the following statement:

Ultimate concern is ultimate risk and ultimate courage. It is not risk and needs no courage with respect to ultimacy itself. But it is risk and demands courage if it affirms a concrete concern. And every faith has a concrete element in itself. It is concerned about something or somebody. But this something or this somebody may prove to be not ultimate at all. Then faith is a failure in its concrete expression, although it is not a failure in the experience of the unconditional itself. A god disappears; divinity remains. Faith risks the vanishing of the concrete god in whom it believes. It may well be that with the vanishing of the god the believer breaks down without being able to re-establish his centered self by a new content of his ultimate concern. This risk cannot be taken away from any act of faith (DF, 18).

Thus whether the symbol of one's faith is Christ, Buddha, the nation, or success, the real possibility of the symbol being, or becoming, idolatrous cannot be precluded from the act of faith.

The tendency toward idolatry present in every faith and the impossibility of knowing whether a given faith will actually become idolatrous make the task of evaluating faiths extremely difficult. How, for example, can one judge the relative merit of Christianity over Judaism, Buddhism, or Islam? The simple division of faiths into objectively true and idolatrous will not do here. Tillich certainly does not hold that only the Christian faith is objectively true.

Tillich, as a Christian theologian, does wish to say something about the intrinsic superiority of the Christian faith and its basic symbol, Jesus as the Christ. But how is this possible? What would constitute the superiority of one faith to another? Once it is admitted that the Buddha, as well as the Christ, is a *genuine* symbol of the divine, what criteria can be employed to distinguish these faiths and determine the Christian faith as superior? Tillich's answer to these questions—perhaps, more exactly, my *interpretation* of Tillich's answer—is that one live faith may be superior to another in either of two ways: (1) the quality of the material constituting the symbol of the one faith may be more suitable for mediating the ultimate; (2) the one faith may be less likely to be or become idolatrous than the other faith. Tillich speaks of these points as *criteria* for determining the degree or amount of truth a faith or a symbol possesses.[4] Point 2 is discussed in all of his writings on religious symbols and clearly occupies a position of fundamental importance in his argument for the superiority of the Christ symbol. Point 1 is mentioned only infrequently.

Concerning 1—which Tillich refers to as the *positive* criterion for judging the worth or degree of objective truth of a symbol—he remarks:

The other criterion is the quality of their symbolic material. There is a difference whether they use trees and rocks and stones and animals or personalities and groups as symbolic material. Only in the last case do the symbols comprise the whole of reality; for only in man are all dimensions of the encountered world united. It is therefore decisive for the rank and value of a symbol that its symbolic

---

[4] Paul Tillich, "The Meaning and Justification of Religious Symbols," *Religious Experience and Truth*, ed. Sidney Hook (New York: New York University Press, 1961), p. 10.

material is taken from the human person. Therefore the great religions are concentrated on a personal development in which ultimate concern appears and transcends the personal limits, though remaining in a person.[5]

Although the reasoning may be obscure, it is clear that Tillich's conclusion here is that a faith whose vehicle of the ultimate is a human person is superior to one in which the ultimate is manifested in a stone, tree, or animal. Thus on the basis of this criterion, Christian faith may be judged superior to the pagan religions whose symbols were animals and other non-human objects.

Concerning 2—which Tillich refers to as the *negative* criterion for judging the worth of a symbol—he remarks:

It is the danger and almost unavoidable pitfall of all religious symbols that they bring about a confusion between themselves and that to which they point. In religious language this is called idolatry. . . . When, however, the symbols are in power their idolatrous misuse is almost unavoidable. The symbol of the "Cross of the Christ," which is the center of all Christian symbolism, is perhaps the most radical criticism of all idolatrous self-elevation. But even it has become again and again the tool of idolatry within the Christian churches. This consideration is the answer to the question of the truth of religious symbols from the negative point of view. The measure of their truth is the measure of their self-negation with respect to what they point to, the Holy-Itself, the ultimate power of being and meaning.[6]

According to Tillich the chief symbol of the Christian faith, Jesus as the Christ, contains its own negation, says of itself, as it were, that it is a *bearer* of the ultimate, and not to be confused with the ultimate. It is this element of self-negation, which Tillich sees in the story of the cross, that constitutes, for him, the superiority of Christian faith over all other religious faiths. "That symbol is most adequate

---

[5] *Ibid.*, p. 11.   [6] *Ibid.*, pp. 10–11.

which expresses not only the ultimate but also its own lack of ultimacy. Christianity expresses itself in such a symbol in contrast to all other religions, namely, in the Cross of the Christ" (DF, 97). Again, he remarks:

Religion is ambiguous and every religious symbol may become idolatrous. . . . If Christianity claims to have a truth superior to any other truth in its symbolism, then it is the symbol of the cross in which this is expressed, the cross of the Christ. He who himself embodies the fullness of the divine's presence sacrifices himself in order not to become an idol, another god beside God, a god into whom the disciples wanted to make him. And therefore the decisive story is the story in which he accepts the title "Christ" when Peter offers it to him. He accepts it under the one condition that he has to go to Jerusalem to suffer and to die, which means to deny the idolatrous tendency even with respect to himself. This is at the same time the criterion of all other symbols, and it is the criterion to which every Christian church should subject itself (TC, 67).

We must not overemphasize Tillich's claims for the superiority of Christian faith over all other religious faiths. He is not, as we saw, maintaining that all other faiths are idolatrous. He is maintaining that Christian faith is superior to any faith whose symbolic material is not drawn from the level of the human person. But, in terms of this criterion, Buddhism, for example, enjoys the same superiority. In the end, his claim for the superiority of the symbol of the Christ over, say, the symbol of the Buddha is that the former expresses an element of self-negation that the latter does not. Now *if* the symbol itself—rather than the group for whom it is a symbol—were the efficient cause of idolatry, this feature of self-negation perhaps would be as important as Tillich undoubtedly believes it to be. That is, if the symbol elevated itself to ultimacy (how could a stone, or a tree do that?), instead of being elevated to ultimacy by the group for which it is a symbol, then it would be highly significant to note that in the story of the cross—as interpreted by Tillich—Jesus as the Christ refused to make himself into an idolatrous symbol of the divine. But becoming idolatrous is something that happens to the symbol when the group comes to view it as inherently holy. And, as Tillich seems to note, the fact that the Christ symbol implies an element of self-negation has not prevented people from making Christ into an idol. "The symbol of the 'Cross of Christ,' which is the center of all Christian symbolism, is perhaps the most radical criticism of all idolatrous self-elevation. But even it has become again and again the tool of idolatry within the Christian churches." Of course, one can argue that the fact that the Christ symbol implies its own negation may make it a less likely candidate for idolatry than, say, the symbol of the Buddha. But one suspects that if the human mind is a continuously working factory of idols—as Tillich, following Calvin, seems to believe—then it is not likely to be put off by the fact that the symbol warns against its idolatrous misuse.

Thus Tillich's claims concerning the superiority of the Christ symbol do not, I think, mark any very profound difference between Christianity and the other great religions by which men live. In view of his conception of God as being-itself and his general theory of religious symbols, I submit that this conclusion should come as no surprise.

Index

Alston, William P., 17, 20–21, 134–36, 183, 192
Anxiety, 18
Aquinas, Thomas, 32, 78–79, 81–83
Aristotle, 57–58
Augustine, 90

Barth, Karl, 5–6
Being: basic transcendental, 59; not the highest genus, 55–59. *See also* Being-itself
Being-itself: argument for the reality of, 86–87; beyond limitations, 35; connection with the holy, 153–70; difficulty of specifying, 134–36; distinguished from the One, 70–72; ineffable, 41; interpreted as Plotinus' the One, 62–71; interpreted as a universal, 43–62; meaning of 'being-itself', 38–41; not the highest universal, 61–62; participation of beings in, 36; statements about must be symbolic, 182, 193; the statement 'God is being-itself', 24–31; thought based on, 83–84; what religious symbols point to, 132–39

Beings: subject to limitations, 35–36
Brown, D. Mackenzie, 237

Christ: and the historical Jesus, 213–15
Coffey, P., 59–60
Copleston, F. C., 78

Edwards, Paul, 183, 190–92

Faith: and historical skepticism, 213–14; criteria for evaluating, 238–42; element of certainty in, 167; element of risk in, 167; idolatrous, 223; objectively true, 223, 235–36; subjectively true, 222, 234–35; truth of, 222
Findlay, J. N., 8
Freud, Sigmund, 210–11
Fundamentalism, 3–4

Gilson, E., 79
God: arguments for the existence of, 87–92; as a religious symbol, 172–75; as concrete, 33, 37, 127–28; as living, 183; as omnipotent, 183; as ultimate, 34; beyond essence and

existence, 61–62; discourse about, 41–42; double meaning of 'God', 175; existence implied, 82–83; meaning of 'God exists', 73–75; object of concern, 13; religious aspect of, 11; religious man's view of, 174–75; tension in the idea of, 33–35, 128

Idolatry: different characterizations of, 230–31; idolatrous symbol, 226; naïve conception of, 224; relation between the symbol and the holy, 227–30; risk of faith and, 237

Liberalism, 3–4

Matthews, Shailer, 5
Metaphysical ultimate, 17. See also Being-itself
Moore, G. E., 154, 159–60
Myths: connection with symbols, 197; fall of Adam, 199–201, 202–6; problems of interpreting and understanding, 199–201

Neo-orthodoxy, 5–6
Nominalism: Tillich's rejection of, 53–55
Nonbeing: related to being-itself, 71; source of anxiety, 18–19

Otto, Rudolf, 146, 156–58

Participation: as an ontological element, 117–19; as a relation between symbols and what they symbolize, 111–16
Plotinus: concept of the One, 62–71
Psychological ultimate, 17

Religion: definition of, 140–41
Religious statements: elucidated by metaphysical statements, 37–38; problem of elucidating, 41–42. *See also* Religious symbols
Religious symbols: and appearances of the divine, 194; cannot be reduced to nonsymbolic language, 182; central problems of, 186–87; classification of, 196; contrasted with traditional view of, 177–80; criticisms of, 183–86; immanent level, 171, 194; manifest the holy, 226–27; objective way of distinguishing, 130–39; phenomenological approach to their referent, 144–46; primary, 172; referent of, 143; statements about God's qualities and actions, 180; subjective way of distinguishing, 130, 139–42; transcendent level, 171
Religious truth: distinguished from historical truth, 211–18; distinguished from philosophical truth, 218–21; distinguished from scientific truth, 207–11; objective side, 222; subjective side, 222

Signs: analysis of, 110; conventional, 108; linguistic, 102; natural, 108–9; point beyond themselves, 102–7; replaceable by other signs, 110–11
Stace, W. T., 190
Symbols: distinguished from signs, 119–24; partial analysis of, 124; participate in what they symbolize, 111–16; point beyond themselves, 102–7; religious symbols distin-

guished, 129–30. *See also* Religious symbols

Theology: method of correlation, 6–7; purpose of, 1–2

Ultimate concern: ambiguity of 'ultimate concern', 20–21; and being-itself, 14–15, 17–21; concrete content of, 16; definition of, 22; experienced by everyone, 148–49; object of experienced as holy, 12–13; requires a concrete content, 150–53; two meanings of distinguished by Tillich, 165

Universals: as predicable, 45; contrasted with particulars, 44; extra-mental existence of, 46–47; neither spatially nor temporally located, 46

Urban, Wilbur M., 25–27

Weiman, Henry Nelson, 5